THE

CHANGEOVER

By

Dr. Lyle Hotchkiss

DEDICATION

Louise Long
(1920-2004)

I dedicate this book to my mother, educator Louise Hotchkiss Long, who incessantly preached to her students—and especially to me—that in order to be highly regarded by others, and to own a positive self-image, it is essential that a person be both honorable and considerate.

AUTHOR'S NOTE REGARDING PRONOUN GENDER

My early educators taught that when gender was unknown, *he, him,* and *his* were to be used as gender-non-specific pronouns in order to prevent a script from being encumbered by an excessive use of *he or she* and *his or hers* throughout a text. My apology goes out to those who believe that my use of this traditional style is sexist. For any who are offended by this political incorrectness, he or she has my permission to mentally substitute the pronouns of his or her choice.

NOT FOR EVERYONE

The Changeover is common sense put into a form that, hopefully, promotes new realizations. Its purpose is to improve the lives of its readers by lessening common depression, anxiety, fear, stress, and frustration. It is meant for those who have the ability to see things logically, and who have sufficient positive energy to apply the book's suggestions. These chapters are not intended to solve the problems of those who suffer from psychological disorders that require medical treatment or that cannot be improved by way of enlightenment.

Contents

Introduction: Moments

A dear friend of mine, Sandy W., is the most positive person I have ever met. Her thinking is structured around the following adages:

If you want to be truly happy,

look for the positives in each day.

and

To get the most out of life,

you must live in the moment.

If you visit Sandy's home, you won't find these words framed and hung over a fireplace or taped to her refrigerator, because Sandy's attitude isn't dependent on motivational reminders. A positive attitude is the core of who she is.

Sandy has been tested time and time again by situations that have had the power to build layers of courage and stamina, but that also have held the potential to fatigue and to destroy. Whereas some people would collapse and stay down for the count, Sandy has been able to absorb punches and keep fighting. Sandy takes refuge in positives, and she refuses to let negative whirlpools suck her in. She has no time for depression because she keeps her calendar filled with possibilities.

How did she achieve this mindset? What makes Sandy so different from those who solve their problems by jumping off bridges? It certainly isn't that her troubles haven't been significant; they just haven't had the negative impact that one would expect.

You might think, *She's just one of the lucky ones*, but luck has nothing to do with owning a positive nature. Constructive or destructive, a mindset is something that's developed over time. It's the result of one's mental programming, not one's fate.

A person's happiness is determined by how he experiences his time. Unfortunately, few enjoy their moments as they should. Far too many race through life only to reach the finish line wondering, *Where did it all go?* When time passes by too quickly, even life's best moments cannot be properly savored. Because time can only be spent, not saved, how we spend our time determines what we get out of it. When our time is spent unfocused or too little significance is placed on what's happening, that time is pretty much wasted. It certainly isn't life enriching.

Instead of fully appreciating what each day has to offer, many believe they need "special" occasions to achieve that longed-for, "special" happiness. Instead of experiencing a consistent plateau of good feelings, they experience peaks and valleys. It's impossible to feel complete when a life is riddled with voids. If your happiness blooms primarily on weekends and holidays, that means you are spending most of your precious moments just passing time, waiting for a better moment to arrive.

Significant moments are what make life significant. Ideally, you should find significance in every precious second, but this isn't possible, of course. There's a limit to what a mind can assimilate, and a moment passes by too quickly. What you can experience, however, is a significant increase in the number of those perceived "special" moments. The more good times you experience, the less room you have for negative thoughts and voids.

If you think about it, there are no insignificant moments, only unappreciated ones. Everything that happens to you is significant, for all those experiences comprise your time, your life.

A significant moment is not necessarily pleasant or momentous. In fact, difficulties make the biggest impact, since negatives breed the strongest emotions. Because they exert such an impression, unpleasant incidents can needle you long after they have dissipated. The mere memory of a negative occurrence can bring back the identical stress that the event originally generated.

It's understandable that people would try to discount the importance of difficult times. Misfortune isn't compatible with happiness. But, when negative moments are written off, the result is a conscious and subconscious masking of some very significant happenings. Significant negatives that become artificially relabeled as "insignificant" can create considerable inner turmoil, especially when those disregarded negatives remain unresolved.

It's human nature to attempt the erasure of unpleasant memories, but this isn't possible. The most that can be achieved is a memory reprogramming that selectively either bypasses or fast forwards over undesirable thoughts and feelings. Skipping over thoughts you want to avoid doesn't mean they have been successfully vanquished. At best, they remain cancers in remission. But even if you could completely eliminate them, you shouldn't. Your traumatic experiences are important facets of who you are.

In fact, a negative state of mind can have a positive effect. A recent study revealed that negative moods are beneficial, because they make us less likely to make wrong decisions than when we are in positive moods, which are the times when we are most likely to act impulsively and make mistakes. That's probably true, but I would much rather be happy and make a few errors than to be unhappy and make no mistakes at all.

To me, the more beneficial aspect of a negative state of mind is that those times, especially the crises, are preeminent opportunities for inner growth. I'm not referring to the traditional perceived benefit that those times are worthwhile because they build character, however. What I submit is that the stressful times are among the best times to discover new positives, positives that otherwise would remain hidden. A durable, positive outlook does not happen by eschewing the tough moments or by pretending you are not affected. It happens by embracing life's inherent difficulties, exposing the positives within, and then turning those situations inside-out by way of enlightenment.

Every now and then in this writing I will be relating bits and pieces of my own beliefs and experiences. It's recommended that non-fiction authors limit their use of the egotistical "I" and "me" in their script, especially in works that aren't autobiographical, but this isn't the usual self-help composition. *The Changeover* is entirely about intimate, personal thoughts, both yours and mine. It's written to be a communication, rather than a textbook. Through this face-to-face style, I hope to connect with you, the person I imagine you to be: a person with the same needs as I and every other human soul.

I decided to write this book to share with you the valuable insight I received as a result of a personal tragedy that redefined my life. Prior to that event I perceived my life as being quite idyllic, with everything pretty much going my way. That security came to an abrupt end when I fell from my protective nest and landed upside-down in a situation that stole every bit of my happiness. My perspective became dark, and I easily could have self-destructed because relief seemed intolerably far away.

You know what? The tragedy that could have cost me the ultimate price ended up being my lifesaver. From it grew the revelation that my interpretations were weak and inadequate to sustain me during times when the road I traveled became rutted. In the process of deeply examining my belief system, I became aware of the frailty of my personal definitions. That insight motivated me to improve my interpretations and understanding of the world around me. Instead of fine-tuning my existing database, I decided it needed a complete changeover. As a result of that mental restructuring, I found an incredible peace, and for the first time in my life I experienced a durable, positive mental attitude that was able to resist being blown about by stormy winds.

My life once revolved around the setting and achievement of goals, all motivated by a hunger for "special" moments. I placed so much emphasis on visualization and planning that much of my world was fiction. Now I understand that I had been dreaming more than living. Since my changeover, I awaken each day realizing that *this* moment matters the most, and it's the present moment that deserves most of my energy.

It might sound as though I've become a realist who no longer dreams, but that's not the case. My dreams haven't stopped. As a matter fact, I still identify with my long-time friend, one of the greatest dreamers of all, Cervantes' Don Quixote. Like that enigmatic knight-errant, I see things differently, not necessarily the way of the masses, and that's how I like it. I admit I occasionally imagine windmill giants that I must be battle, and I can't resist chasing impossible dreams. Some may see folly in my actions, but I've chosen not to let contrary perspectives deter me from my quest.

Dreams have their merit, even though they are fabrications. Dreams can provide relief from a sometimes harsh and unjust world by their ability to give hope for a better reality to come. A dream of honesty, truth, fairness, courage, good over evil, and success against all odds can inspire one to keep persevering. Dreams augment reality when they enhance the true moment. They become negatives only if they are substitutes for today's positive harvest. No, my dreams and goals have not lessened; they just no longer are my primary focus.

***

At an early stage of composing *The Changeover*, my heart became heavily laden. I received word that my sister, Sandra Lee, had been given only two more weeks to live. It was only a year before when her doctor found she had inoperable cancer. For Sandra, the trials of life were soon to end.

My sister had endured an inordinate number of tough times throughout her life, but, unlike with Sandy W., my sister never seemed able to surmount those obstacles. Sandra Lee viewed day-to-day routine as an adversary, and for her that made consistent happiness a truly impossible dream.

During her healthy years, Sandra did experience many good moments, especially during holidays and family celebrations, but in order for a moment to meet her expectations, she had to make it a "special" event, always requiring a great deal of orchestration and self-sacrifice. By and large, satisfaction remained elusive to her. Fortunately, she had the love of a close-knit family to sustain her through those frequent disappointments.

I had planned to present my sister with an early draft of this book, hoping it would inspire a sense of peace during the time she had left. Long before the completion of this work, however, Sandra Lee passed away. Although this writing wasn't finished in time for her eyes, she was an inspiration to help me communicate ideas that I now hope will foster the betterment of *your* life.

My present goal is to help you rebuild the foundation of your thinking so that you too can have greater fulfillment. Contrary to what you may expect, you will not be persuaded to adopt my perspective, and you will not be told what you should think. Instead, you'll learn a process that, once personalized, will enable you to write your own story of success. The intent of *The Changeover* is to clarify your world and its indoctrinations, so that you will then be able to understand why you think and feel the way you do. After misconceptions have been brought to light, it will teach you how to intentionally reprogram your mind, so that you will achieve a new, healthier perspective from which to enjoy living.

If you glean nothing more from this writing, I hope you'll become attuned to the overwhelming importance of being dedicated to the moment. After all, moments are all you have. Moments that pass by unappreciated are blank pages in your life story, but moments that are appreciated fill your story with script. Although you may not realize it, you have begun your own composition. What will be written hereafter is up to you, and it will be done by your own hand. You can write an exciting page-turner, or two out of three pages can be empty. Bare pages obviously make for a boring story. What will you write?

PART I: ACHIEVEMENT

1
The Changeover

You've seen makeovers on television and in magazines. Now it's your turn for a transformation. But this one will be more than a cosmetic fix; this one will permanently alter your vision of life, especially how you view yourself. Instead of a temporary makeover, it will be a durable changeover. You will soon revamp your thinking to achieve contentment greater than you ever thought possible. You are beginning what just might prove to be your greatest personal accomplishment.

If you already feel contented, you will learn how to reach even greater heights of satisfaction through a growth in appreciation, patience, tolerance, peace, and love. If you are experiencing a state of depression, you will learn how to rise above it by becoming the master of negative impulses. No matter what your state of mind, your life will soon become better.

I'm ready to improve myself, improve my life.

None of us will ever be the best we can be. We are each a portrait-in-progress, forever an incomplete work hungering for more brush strokes. You know this, of course, or you wouldn't be reading this book. Your interest in self-improvement shows that you are aware that your painting is not yet finished. Even if your purpose for reading these pages is merely to add scenery to the good feelings you already have, you know there is more you can do.

You would like to always look and feel your best, right? With sufficient discretionary funds, you can have better teeth, thicker hair, a smaller tummy, and even a new nose. Add such cosmetic enhancements to a healthy diet with regular exercise, and it's possible to significantly improve your appearance. But what about your emotional state? What about feeling better? There is little benefit in looking your best if you are not also feeling your best.

When you feel inadequate, your inclination is to look at yourself, rather than into yourself, but your feelings emanate from a soul, not an image. At most, changing your surface can only change the surface of how you feel. Although your mirror may reveal superficial imperfections that trouble you, perceived cosmetic deficiencies are never at the root of a darkened state of mind. Negative feelings are the result of far more complicated issues.

To significantly improve your attitude, attention must be focused on correcting your internal flaws. This requires making structural changes. Motivational cheerleading can only temporarily quell deep-rooted negativity. A lasting, positive changeover does not happen by implementing techniques that are merely inspirational. Layering positive messages over an imperfect psychological foundation is no different than applying makeup to blemishes, or spraying paint over rusted steel. You may temporarily feel better by using a positive determination to mask your problems, but wouldn't you rather permanently improve your attitude? By applying the suggestions presented in *The Changeover*, you will soon do just that.

I'm told that I can be whatever I want to be, but I can't envision being anything different.

You cannot become more positive and your life cannot be made better until you restructure your thinking. In order for your imagination to envision new possibilities, it must be freed from its enslavement. You must escape the limitations that you have been placing on yourself.

There is truth behind the sayings, "You can't teach an old dog new tricks" and "People never really change." There are good reasons for your present thoughts, and for how you react to the various situations that confront you. Over time you have developed a powerful belief system that controls these responses. Your inner guide has become your inner dictator. Anything you attempt to do that goes against this belief system will eventually end in defeat. In order for your perceptions to become significantly different from what they are now, you must reconstruct that belief system. It must be converted into one that helps you, not one that holds you back.

I'd like to restructure my thinking, but how do I know what changes to make?

Your own personal needs will guide you. Your objective is not to become a clone, it is to become *you*. There is no single, prescribed model to emulate. What works for most others might not be comfortable for you, and the rough road in someone else's belief system might be your freeway. Your goal isn't to exchange your present mode of thinking for thoughts that another person believes you should have. Your goal is just the opposite. Your personal mission is to replace other peoples' persuasions with your own realizations. *Becoming you* is the key!

Most of your beliefs are not your own creation; they are the result of indoctrinations. Your reactions to all life happenings have been influenced, and even predetermined, by the prejudiced opinions of others, primarily those of your parents and your earliest role models. A belief is not your own unless you have given personal consideration to the facts that comprise it. To have confidence in the correctness of your beliefs, you must test them yourself, rather than relying on the hand-me-down assumptions and biases of those who have been your teachers.

In order to establish strong, sincere beliefs that can be depended upon, your beliefs must be founded entirely on truth, and in order for those beliefs to inspire a consistently positive attitude, the majority of those truths must be positive in nature.

When positive truths are the primary components of your thought processing, they will invariably generate a consistently positive attitude toward life as a whole. Honest, positive beliefs are essential for durable, positive results.

I'd like to have a positive attitude, but I don't see many positives around me.

Positives are never readily apparent when one is in a negative state of mind. That doesn't mean they do not exist. You may not be able to see them, but positives are everywhere, even hidden within your negative perceptions. You will find them if you look for them.

Many consider Sanibel Island to be the world's shelling capital. I know those white sand beaches well, and have spent many hours combing the shoreline, looking for beautiful shells to augment my collection. There are times on Sanibel when the shells are so thickly mounded along the water's edge that it's difficult to walk barefoot without shredding the soles of my feet. You would think this abundance would make it easy to find whatever type of shell I happen to be looking for, but when there are thousands upon thousands to peruse, an individual species easily blends in with the masses. However, it seems that if I truly dedicate myself to finding Tulip shells, I find Tulip shells. If I look only for Whelks, I find Whelks. When I pre-program my brain to spot a specific type of shell, I am more apt to find precisely what I am seeking.

The same holds true when accumulating facts to support a state of mind. If you look for negatives, negatives are what you will discover. If you make a decision to search for positives, they will be revealed to you. It's entirely up to you which state of mind you embrace, and which supporting facts you collect.

If your state of mind consistently promotes good feelings, that indicates you have acquired a healthy collection of facts. If your thoughts are too frequently negative, or if your disposition fluctuates significantly, your collection is unhealthy. Regardless of your state of mind, collecting positive perceptions will make you happier. However, adding new, positive perceptions doesn't undo the preexisting data that controls the majority of your thoughts. To establish an improved attitude that is durable, you must build a healthier foundation on which to interpret life; you must freshen your perspective.

2

"Mirror, Mirror…"

Even though mirrors can be cruel, they are fascinating. Few people can pass by one without sneaking a peek. We are each intrigued by our own image, especially how we appear to others. A mirror provides that vantage. Mirrors allow you to step outside yourself and examine what others see, helping you to better define who you are by adding an image to your thoughts and feelings. With the aid of your reflection, you are better informed than when your appearance is only imagined.

Better informed? Yes. Accurately judged? Not likely. Each of us is biased, especially when self-evaluating. It's not possible to be completely objective when considering your own image. Your nature is to either overlook or to accentuate your "imperfections." You see what you choose to see, not what truly exists.

It would seem, then, that asking someone else to evaluate your appearance would prove to be more accurate than making a self-appraisal, but outsiders also have biases that work to distort the facts, and even if someone with the capability to make a disciplined, unadulterated judgment were to be found, could you trust that person to be entirely forthright in sharing that evaluation with you? A person will usually hesitate to offer a candid assessment when there's a possibility that it would injure another person's self-esteem. Therefore, when it comes to obtaining an accurate appraisal of your appearance, you are left doing a lot of guesswork: guessing what others truly think when they look at you, and guessing what your own conclusions should be.

Of course, there is much more to knowing yourself than can be deduced by studying your image. The greater challenge is to understand your mind. Once again, this is a realm where personal objectivity is impossible, and with no one else able to experience exactly what you think and feel, any outside opinion must rely primarily on assumptions of what is actually taking place. Since such conclusions are speculative, any psychological analysis is an endeavor laced with guesses, regardless of who is doing it.

Still, you owe it to yourself to do the best you can. The more complete your understanding of why you think and act as you do, the more your life will make sense. Understanding your reasoning is the prerequisite for spiritual freedom, and the fewer questions you have about yourself, the better equipped you are to attend to the business of routine living.

Inner confusion is a blockade to both your self-actualization and your ability to relish the moment, thus your foremost goal should be to achieve a mental atmosphere that "has it together." Throughout your life you have been advised what to do. Here are some of those words:

Think positive thoughts.

Live for today.

Don't worry about the future.

Change what you cannot accept;

accept what you cannot change.

Be appreciative.

Take time to smell the roses.

Exercise both your mind and body.

Stay busy.

Make the best of each situation.

Don't dwell on the past.

Live and let live.

Keep your priorities straight.

Look on the bright side.

Keep the faith.

You have no doubt heard these adages time and time again, and you know they are true, yet they probably have done very little for you. That's because you are most receptive to inspirational messages during the moments when you are already feeling quite good—in other words, when they are least needed. When you are at you lowest, such phrases rarely come to mind.

Motivational messages typically can't penetrate the armor of a negative mental state. If they could, more people would be content with whatever cards they've been dealt. To be a truly positive person, you must program your mind to spontaneously form its own positive messages. A positive inclination must be your default program. It needs to be your modus operandi, not just a temporary attitude for dealing with whatever happens to be ailing you at the moment.

It's not possible to achieve a personal philosophy that engenders a dependable, positive energy by merely absorbing someone else's words of wisdom. Such an aura can only be born of your own wisdom. This doesn't happen by inseminating a good intent; it happens by developing *honest* positive beliefs.

I emphasize "honest," because happiness can't be contrived. In fact, it's counterproductive to continually work at being happy. If you must make personal sacrifices in order for good moments to occur, then achieving happiness is as stressful a process as any other chore in life. Authentic happiness necessitates thoughts that contribute to your well-being without fostering anxiety. Feeling good should be easy and natural. No sacrifice. Effortless.

For something to have a lasting, positive effect on your state of mind, it must be compatible with it. It's imperative, then, that you understand the information that your gray matter has absorbed, and also that you find out why you have interpreted that information the way you have. You must understand your inner workings before you can know what improvements to make. The precursor to a better life is solving that mystery in your mirror.

Standing in front of a mirror aids self-evaluation, but what is perceived can be enlightening in more ways than simply the provision of visual data. A perception can reveal a great deal more, especially if it leads to contemplation. By blending both your surface impression and deeper introspection, it's possible to utilize all of a mirror's messages and journey beyond the realm of what seems obvious, to the ultimate determinant of all your interpretations: *your perspective.*

What do you see when you look in the mirror?

Is the image connected with you: something sharing your innermost feelings, an extension of your soul?

or

Do you see an example of all humanity: something less connected, belonging to a less personal whole?

A person's interpretations are determined by the perspective that is being utilized. There are two distinct types that are commonly used. One of these looks at things intimately, with what I can best describe as an *emotional* point of view. The other analyzes from a distance, with more of a *logical* point of view. The first one examines the world quite subjectively, the second one more objectively. Each functions by itself, independently of the other, even though they work for the same mind. Consequently, a person's interpretations can vary greatly, depending on which type of perspective happens to be dominant at any given moment.

An *emotional perspective* makes its interpretations with a point of view that is heavily influenced by feelings. This perspective seeks personal gratification. It chooses self-preservation over self-sacrifice, so it would rather make love, not war. It has a narrow vision. This perspective will dismiss a diet for the immediate pleasure of a hot fudge sundae. It's the perspective responsible for jittery nerves when sitting in a waiting room.

A *logical perspective* rarely runs on emotion. It operates with an omniscient train of thought. This perspective is rewarded by accomplishment and by doing the right thing. It encourages self-sacrifice for the attainment of a goal, and it has excellent peripheral vision. Someone with this perspective has the sense to reject a juicy bratwurst for the sake of a lower cholesterol level, yet will voluntarily risk life and limb for "the good of the whole."

There are those whose perspectives are predominantly either *emotional* or *logical*, with some taking everything to heart, and others taking things only for what they are worth. Most people, however, have perspectives that are a blending of these two influences, combined with an intermingling of hundreds of lesser, rogue perspectives on every topic from politics to fiddlesticks.

You cannot function with any consistency if you must contend with multiple perspectives, each of which is determined to be in charge. The more choices you have to consider, the greater the likelihood that you will occasionally make judgmental errors. You don't need this confusion!

The more consistent your thinking, the clearer your course. Therefore, the wise thing to do is to replace those competing viewpoints with a single, well-balanced perspective. It's possible to select a comfortable philosophical base, and then use it to launch a pre-designed perspective that determines how all information is processed. This is far better than allowing your mood to be dictated by an unpredictable, "perspective of the day."

Putting a single perspective in charge brings consistency to one's vision, but in order for that perspective to make reliable interpretations, it must be supported by reliable information. In general, learning occurs in a very haphazard fashion. The huge body of information that you have absorbed throughout your life has come from a multitude of sources, with each adding its own philosophical warp and each presenting its facts as accurate, even if they were not. Without realizing it, you have formed strong opinions based on all those "facts," and, unfortunately, the majority of those acquired definitions have been tenuously founded on trust rather than on confirmations of the truth. Your mind has stored this accurate and inaccurate data, resulting in an archive that encompasses many varied (often conflicting) interpretations. There has been no plan, no order, no uniformity, and no consistency. There have been plenty of assumptions. Your database is an assemblage of individual-yet-intertwining beliefs that meander hither and yon through your thinking process like cows randomly grazing through a pasture.

Having an intricate database is a good thing up to a point. It provides a vast archive of information from which to draw, and it contributes to your uniqueness as an individual. But, when contradictory facts accumulate beyond your ability to properly sort them out, you then have a problem.

Consider this visualization:

It's relatively easy to process the body of images that appear on a television screen. Even if the scenes are action-packed, a mind can usually keep up with the pace. A little more difficult is the viewing of a TV set with the picture-in-picture feature activated. With this capability it's possible to view two separate programs at the same time, although not without missing a few details from either one.

The ultimate test of boob-tube acuity happens when standing in front of an entire wall of TV monitors at the local electronics megastore. At these places it's possible to view multiple broadcasts simultaneously. For a while (about ten seconds), this effect can be pleasantly surreal, but a brain must eventually escape such chaos to avoid blowing its fuse.

There is a method to view many screens at once and still be considerate to your brain: It's possible to take a group of monitors and configure them as a unit, so that they together present a single image the size of an entire wall. Rather than working independently, they can be linked together to enhance a viewer's perception.

The point I wish to make is that an individual thought, reasonable by itself, has the power to disturb reasoning ability when thrown in with contradictory thoughts. An individual thought that is compatible with other thoughts strengthens their net effect. As contradictions and inconsistencies increase, the clarity of one's thinking diminishes. As the proportion of compatible thoughts grows, mental acuity improves.

The first thing you must do to achieve a significantly improved state of well-being is to begin wading through your established presumptions and beliefs, weeding and thinning them until the only ones that remain are those that best define you, and those that you feel are most important. These are the core items you will then build upon. Your task is to discover which beliefs are truly yours, and which actually belong to someone else. You can then assemble your realizations into a compatible whole that clarifies and, most importantly, simplifies how you view life.

After sorting these things out, will you find that you are predominantly *emotional*? *Logical*? A mixture of both? Are you willing to look into a mirror and discover, among all the expressions and possibilities that are reflected back, who you really are? Are you willing to listen to what that mirror tells you, trust its message, and then give it your full attention?

This changeover is entirely about self. You have been taught that it's not nice to put yourself first, but whether it seems politically correct or not, it is a fact that you are the center of everything that you experience, and that makes you inherently egoistic (self-interested). Of course, it would be repugnant to be egocentric (excessively self-interested), especially at the expense of another person's happiness, but to have good mental health with the capacity to make a worthwhile social contribution, you must attend to yourself first. A determination to improve oneself is an honorable quest, for becoming a better person not only feels good, it also makes the world better.

It's critical that you hone a healthy self, so that you can absorb life, rather than merely being an observer of it. Where do you begin? You begin by learning more about your core being, especially about what really matters to you. But, correctly analyzing your mind's roots is not a simple task, because for most of its life it has traveled down paths that others have said it should take. With a little introspection, you will realize that many of your goals are actually extensions of someone else's goals, and that your interests would likely be different if you had developed without such influences. What if you could begin discovering the world all over again? Isn't it probable that your mind would find new paths to travel, that your likes and dislikes would be different?

All of your life you have been copying others, working on your wish list, and trying to build a comfortable nest for yourself. Feeling materially and emotionally secure has been your priority. But a security that offers comfort without stimulation is not worth much. A nest's purpose is to hold an egg while it matures, and to protect a hatchling until it can fly, not to preclude an egg from ever hatching.

You are probably an egg that has been in the nest too long, just lying there, waiting for the future to unfold. At some point you must decide if you are going to remain inside that shell, forever an embryo, or if you are going to emerge and launch yourself into a world of new possibilities. I'm betting you would rather take flight.

Nothing will ever be different until you become more self-aware. Nothing will improve until you begin listening to your inner voice. To accomplish this changeover you must focus, decide what you need to do, and then do it.

Whether actually or figuratively, begin with a mirror. It is the most honest of all teachers, since it is just you communicating with yourself. Commence the construction of a new perspective by looking deeply into that mirror to disclose realizations that will change things for the better. Your soul (your truest reflection) is anxious to speak. It only asks that you listen.

3
Axes to Axels

You've never been solely responsible for your behavior. Technically, the decision on how to act has been yours alone, but those decisions have been influenced by the thought processes of a multitude of other minds, including those of your parents, Plato, and even Alley-Oop. For a better understanding of why you think and act as you do, let's take a few moments to consider your roots and the environment in which you have been raised.

Human-like creatures have been roaming the Earth for eons. There's evidence to suggest that ancient hominids existed at least fifteen million years ago. However, those earliest ancestors were hardly more than apes until somewhere around two-million B.C., when an improved knuckle-dragger named Homo erectus came on the scene. This hominid was the first to be blessed with both a unique joint configuration that allowed it to walk upright, and a higher intellect that enabled it to create the first rudimentary tools.

Since that era, other pre-humans have come and gone, with all contributing their uniqueness to the hominid chain of life, until *Homo sapiens sapiens* (you and I) finally arrived. We are the latest and greatest link, a species that has ruled supreme over all others for somewhere around two hundred thousand years.

Yes, humans have been in existence for a long, long time—plenty of time to develop consistent patterns of behavior. Nevertheless, our enduring nature hasn't resulted in our being predictable. Humans are not like the other creatures; our ability to make long-range plans and achieve them via goals has set us apart.

For instance, there is probably little difference between the behavior of a pride of lions today and that of lions living two hundred thousand years ago, as these animals are instinctive creatures who act spontaneously according to their immediate needs. The necessities that lions require on a day-to-day level haven't changed.

Human culture, on the other hand, has undergone a huge metamorphosis. We do more than just react to our environment, because we are able to manipulate it. It isn't surprising that this has resulted in continual societal transformation throughout the thousands of years we have been around. What is surprising is the recent acceleration of this change.

Within an incredibly short time relative to our entire past, we have progressed from simple, opportunistic individuals who, by the grace of either God or Lady Luck, stumbled upon whatever food and shelter we could find, into a complex, sophisticated civilization. We have amassed the resources and mastered the technologies necessary to afford us the luxury of countless trivial concerns, such as what color of cell phone cover to select, and whether we would prefer paper or plastic grocery bags. Consider the fact that it took around two hundred thousand years—roughly ten thousand generations—for humans to attain the level of progress that was present during the Roman Empire, and then compare it to the extraordinary change since then.

I don't know about you, but when I consider mankind's progress, I don't envision ox carts… I see factories. The most recent one hundred and fifty years fits that image quite well. This period encompasses the Industrial Revolution through today's prolific era of discovery. Selecting this time frame narrows our focus from approximately three thousand consecutive lifetimes to only two or three. Although no more than a few heartbeats on the EKG of mankind, this era has been responsible for an unparalleled increase in knowledge and achievement, stimulating a time of dramatic societal change that was unimaginable just a few centuries ago.

Prior to 1850 we were primarily an agricultural society, with farming the most prevalent occupation. Farm life necessitated large nuclear families wherein each member was expected to contribute to the well-being of all. As in prehistoric times, a strong family unit was a prerequisite for survival.

Industrialization forever altered that strong family unit, the time-tested backbone of civilization. The advent of booming production and retail centers lured thousands away from their farms, with promises of an easier life and greater prosperity. To house these first waves of the urban workforce, homes began being built close to factories and businesses, resulting in an unprecedented concentration of both laborers and entrepreneurs, and as cities grew, families became increasingly segmented.

With industrialization, the traditions of rural life faded quickly, especially once the horse and wagon were retired. The invention and subsequent mass production of the automobile redefined transportation, and enabled city dwellers and countrymen alike to travel far beyond their immediate boundaries. This improved mobility allowed a much greater personal freedom, which, concomitantly, placed additional strain on established customs. It took only a few years for the cohesiveness that had been inherent in families over thousands of years to weaken, and for the traditional family to fade away.

A strong parent/child relationship is the most essential factor for both the assimilation of established family values, and also for maintaining an atmosphere of "family first." Typical modern-day families still exhibit strong, instinctive bonds at their inception, but as time passes, external influences work to pry those bonds apart.

Even when coddled by well-intentioned, first-time parents, today's young children receive dissociated information via baby sitters, playmates, social media, and the myriad of activities that take place away from the home. Kids do best when they are firmly planted in the ground, lovingly cultivated, pruned with discipline, and then allowed to ripen before being harvested by the world. In an environment of working parents, divorced parents, stepparents, single parents, and non-parents, it's tough for many children to find security and substance anywhere. They are like leaves floating down-stream, at the mercy of fate and susceptible to whatever influences they happen to bump into.

However, children aren't the only losers in a complex society, especially when there's so much being offered, yet little of it attainable. With routine living not meeting their expectations, most adults now look outside their personal world for fulfillment, perfectly exemplified by the growing popularity of reality television, which provides vicarious living from the comfort of a La-Z-Boy.

Yes, the last one hundred and fifty years has certainly been an era of exponential change. Many customs that were relied upon for stability and security over thousands of generations have become passé, and our culture is continually being redefined. Who knows what lies ahead? The old adage, "There ain't nothin' new under the sun," doesn't apply anymore. This is a learn-as-we-go time when we have to improvise to solve problems never before encountered.

That's not to say that our quality of life has diminished, however. Many wondrous discoveries have taken place, and it is certain that countless more are on the horizon. Thanks to modern advancements, life in the physical sense continues to get easier. But, increased food productivity, better quality and availability of healthcare, and improved transportation have also stressed society by their contribution to a phenomenal increase in the Earth's population. This is now our greatest societal problem.

Babies are being produced faster than societal solutions. As a result, a critical scenario is emerging: Many developing countries are unable to contain their populace within their own borders, due to unfavorable conditions that are caused by the severe disparity between their booming numbers and shrinking resources. Because of this, huge numbers of legal and illegal immigrants are adding even further to this country's population growth. By the year 2050, it has been estimated that the United States will have a population of almost four hundred million. With our present birth and immigration rates, that number should increase at least another twenty-five percent by the end of this century, with no end in sight. To make matters worse, such predictions don't even take into account the increased lifespan which is certain to come about.

Here is something to ponder: Over the past half-century alone, there have been as many new births in the world as the total number of people who have *ever* been born. That's right . . . throughout mankind's entire existence! This amazing proliferation is affecting both societal needs and worldwide politics. It's responsible for pollution, depletion of natural resources, governments going broke, people rising in rebellion, and the systematic loss of personal freedoms. By numbers alone, each individual is becoming less and less significant.

Nature is an expert at self-regulation. Being at the mercy of the environment, most animal populations are kept in line by the availability of food, by weather conditions, and by calamities such as diseases and natural disasters. These limiting factors provide the give-and-take necessary for species regulation and, ultimately, species survival.

Humans have been the exception. We have made adjustments that other animals haven't been able to make. This has allowed us to escape the natural order, and spread like locusts across the continents. When we numbered only in the millions, the land and its resources seemed inexhaustible. With a population numbering over six billion, we no longer have limitless resources available to us, yet there hasn't been a decline or even a plateau in our proliferation.

The ability to manage the effects of many factors once considered "Acts of God" has enabled some countries to support and sustain much larger populations than what would be dictated by nature alone. Some even produce more than they can consume. When wealthy nations are blessed with an excess bounty, and share it with impoverished cultures in faraway or remote areas of the world, the resources that these less-fortunate people receive feign a natural abundance. By receiving foreign aid, these populations are being artificially sustained, which overrides the natural limitations that would otherwise work to keep their numbers in balance. Therefore, both their population and their dependency keep increasing. In fact, many have become so reliant on others for their existence that should humanitarian aid be withdrawn, they would find themselves in an even worse situation than before help was provided. Their lives float tenuously on the continued prosperity of others.

We are an emotional species, and, from the broadest of perspectives, we are a single, close-knit family. When other humans suffer, we too feel pain. The human aspiration is to minimize strife and maximize happiness. In order to accomplish these things, we strive to control everything possible. We are an egocentric species that has subscribed to the motto, "Any means to an end," since time immemorial, but when we bend the environment to our needs, we are tampering with the natural order.

Prior to the modern era, we didn't have to concern ourselves with the effect of our actions upon the planet. It made little impact when we dammed a stream or killed a few bison. But, in the last 150 years all that has changed. We now have reshaped the earth, built every imaginable structure, and destroyed everything that has stood in our way. We have even begun to trash outer space with our satellites and interplanetary probes. Hooray for "progress!"

As land resources become exhausted, our future may well rest in the vitality of Earth's last frontier, the Sea. Unfortunately, polar ice is disappearing, the oceans are being fouled by contaminants, reefs are dying, and fish populations are diminishing—all this and we are just beginning to realize our potential for environmental abuse. The water surrounding us was once the womb of life; it may well be our last refuge. What will happen when we deplete our oceans as we have our land? Even if we wholeheartedly uphold the belief that we are special in terms of all other life, and that self-preservation must be achieved at any cost, the fact remains: We are causing an essential, natural balance to undergo perilous stress. We are pushing nature (which includes you and I) to its limits and, potentially, into a catastrophic situation.

All these facts have influenced your perspective. They have set the tone for all of your interpretations and resulting feelings. There are numerous reasons to be gravely concerned about what you've just read, but this chapter has not been written to upset you; it has been constructed with a specific, beneficial purpose. The intent is for you to ultimately extract something positive out of all of this. It is vital that you begin observing and understanding more of what's going on around you, so that you see where you are headed and what things are exerting a negative impact on you. It is imperative that you understand things as they really are, not just as you imagine or hope them to be, and that you develop an improved perspective that will bring your deliverance, rather than your subjugation.

4
Battle of Perspectives

Even though your time on Earth may be historically insignificant, these few years are everything you have. Your time limitation is what makes each moment so important. It is the awareness of one's mortality that creates gusto for life and compels one to work diligently to achieve goals as quickly as possible.

Amazing changes can occur within a lifetime, especially in this age of rapid technological growth, but experiencing change also means being challenged. Life would be easier in an unchanging world, for as with a pride of lions, all we would have to do to feel contentment would be to adapt to the periodic ebb and flow, then create the best possible life within those boundaries.

In an ever-changing human world, it's much more difficult to achieve balance. It seems whenever a comfortable station in life is reached, change is forced upon us. We continually are required to adapt and be resourceful in order to solve our problems. These incessant provocations are responsible for the present epidemic of modern-day stress ailments. No one has the time or the ability to relax.

Most people choose one of two approaches for handling each day: 1) They remain flexible, allowing their perspectives and personal definitions to adapt as the need arises; or 2) They hold firmly to their established preferences, and refuse to budge when pulled by new trends and ideas.

Option #1 is the safe approach for someone who does not yet know himself. It's the option favored by the young and inexperienced. Avoiding conflict or being politically correct requires this type of life posture. It may seem somewhat wishy-washy, but it's the logical way to think if you want to be everything to everyone.

Option #2 is the one favored by those who feel they do not fit in with the current fashion, those who are antagonistic toward change. An example would be those senior citizens who finish out their years clinging to old, comfortable definitions, regardless of what's happening around them.

When looked at objectively, both choices are cop-outs, and they are equally self-defeating. So, why do people pick either one? Does it depend on one's age, where each end of the life spectrum produces a philosophy compatible with one's shortcomings? What do you think is the best approach?

The reasons for a person's choices in life can rarely be interpreted objectively, for they are produced subjectively. A personal choice is a difficult thing to evaluate. What may appear on the surface to expose a psychological weakness could, in fact, indicate a psychological strength. The answer lies within the private needs of each individual.

There is no shortage of advice on what to do and how to think. You only have to turn on the radio or pick up a magazine to receive more tips on solving life's problems. By and large, anyone's failure in the matter is not due to lack of information; it is due to lack of application. Too much information can be overwhelming when you are searching for answers, resulting in the experimentation with one technique after another, never bringing the concerted effort necessary to make a real difference.

Wouldn't it be great if all that advice could be condensed and simplified into a single concept that could be easily absorbed, held onto, and carried with you wherever you go? It's possible through your *perspective*. With the creation of a healthy perspective, everything naturally falls into place. Happiness then comes easily and naturally. *Perspective* is the key!

The various perspectives that you presently call upon were many millennia in the making. Both a belief system and a culture were handed to you, and then you personalized them. From your earliest sense of awareness, everything you've heard and experienced has contributed to your own, customized images of how things are and how they should be.

Many of your deductions are sound, but some are flawed because they were founded on falsehoods or misconceptions. The most unreliable of them are the many that formed during your impressionable youth, when you were immature and your ability to evaluate was less astute than it is now. Because your general perspective contains many antiquated images, there's no doubt that it could be improved.

To acquire a perspective that supports you in your quest—whatever that may be—you must begin to reevaluate the foundation upon which that perspective is built. All it takes to commence a fresh start is to open your mind and begin thinking differently. With a little guided introspection, you will soon understand what your real needs are, and what new goals should be set. You will escape the influences of the past and the pull of the masses. You will develop a new Primary Perspective and recreate yourself as a true individual.

Your present mindset is so firmly established that revamping it will in the beginning be like walking through deep, sticky mud. Your first steps need to be strong, sure steps. Even though the "present you" wants to change, the "old you" will resist. To override this reluctance, you must have purpose, have confidence, and act with determination. Old habits and beliefs are webs that entrap you. You must allow those strands to fall away so you'll be free to experience something exciting and new.

In some respects, you are correct if you believe that you have little control over what goes on in the universe. Life's just happening, a continuum of surprises to be lived rather than intellectualized. You're mistaken if you believe that it's possible to make sense of everything, that life can be read and interpreted. You are also mistaken if you believe that there are specific thoughts that you are supposed to have. Happiness is not dependent on everything going according to plan. You don't have to understand all that you see, and you don't have to be in control of the moment. As a matter of fact, experiencing something that you don't quite understand is much more wondrous than experiencing that which you already know well.

Sources for happiness come in many disguises, but these same sources can also hide negative elements. Most everything you experience can be given either a positive or negative slant, depending on your perspective. Here is a short exercise that will help personalize this point:

First, imagine this is a dreary, rainy day. You are in a cemetery, standing alone before the grave of a special loved one who has just passed away. This is a very dark moment in your life. You are heartbroken. Stare at the headstone. Put yourself in a very solemn state of mind. Tune out the world around you as much as you can. Softly close your eyes and allow your heartfelt thoughts and feelings to flow from their innermost recesses. When this image begins to seem real, ask yourself:

Is life really worth living?

(Allow a number of seconds for contemplation.............)

Now that you have gone deeply inside yourself for a few moments, I want you to disregard the question that was asked. Instead take note of the feeling that resulted.

Next, I want you to pretend again, but this time using a different image. I want you to envision the most perfect, sunny day. See yourself standing on a beautiful, grassy hilltop, just like the one Julie Andrews graced when she sang the title song in The Sound of Music. You are surrounded by abundant splendor. Life doesn't get much better than this! As you slowly turn around, your eyes take in a panorama of springtime flowers and snow-capped mountain peaks. Now, take a deep breath of refreshing, cool, alpine air, softly close your eyes, put on a big smile, and ask yourself:

Is life really worth living?

(Again, allow a few seconds for contemplation...............)

What did you feel this time? How did this feeling compare to the one experienced in the previous exercise? I'm sure they were not the same. Even though both questions were identical, the dissimilar situations spawned dissimilar feelings. Can you see how it's possible to give two entirely different answers to the same question, depending on your mindset at any given moment? Your interpretations are almost entirely the result of your perspective.

Your state of mind has more of an influence on your interpretations than do the facts. You are an emotional being who subjectively colors the truth, either positively or negatively, according to your mood and your aspirations, and those personal definitions influence your interpretations thereafter. Rather than expending time and energy to objectively evaluate each new situation that you experience, your efficient mind calls upon past definitions whenever it is required to make new ones. This is how a mindset perpetuates itself.

How eye-opening to realize that what you felt during a specific moment many years ago could still be influencing your thoughts today! If it's possible for your interpretations to vary according to your state of mind at the time, then it's logical to presume that at least some of what now makes up your belief system—your individuality—could be reconsidered. Most likely, your present, overall perspective would improve if you could start afresh with more accurate information and better mental images.

You can't help but be biased when evaluating your surroundings. This is because you have an ego. Your ego is your distinguishable self. It's your ego that separates you from the rest of the pack, but that also makes it difficult for you to have a neutral vision. Your self-oriented way of looking at everything— i.e. "How does it affect me?"— results in a narrow sense of existence and automatic behaviors that cause life to pass by all too quickly.

Your ego's need for fulfillment inspires you to set personal goals which, in turn, manipulate your thoughts and actions much more than you realize. Although you are also manipulated by worldly influences, such as your job and your relationships, you are primarily influenced by restrictions that you self-impose, especially through your aspirations.

The act of selecting a specific goal sets a subconscious, automatic achievement process in motion. Ideas that support your ambition are embraced, while disruptive thoughts are suppressed. The extent to which this self-manipulation is employed depends on how determined you are to achieve your goal. Strong desires, as a rule, tighten your focus. This is great for achieving a goal but not so good for recognizing other opportunities. When you put too much effort into goal achievement, you lose sight of the broader picture, your moments lose their significance, and life speeds up. This is a high price to pay, especially for something that may never be realized.

American society is extremely goal-oriented. We are among the world's leading movers and shakers. We created the assembly line and the power lunch. Why are we like this? Why are we so different from the people of Peru, Samoa, or Nepal? How have we been able to move ahead of civilizations that have preceded us by many centuries, such as the Egyptians, Romans, and Greeks? Do we have better genes? Are we divinely blessed?

The United States is an amalgam of people from all over the world, so there is no common bloodline to support a superior DNA theory. Instead of our biochemistry, then, it must be the chemistry of our society that has set us apart. Rather than being the result of special genes, our successes must have come from special dreams, byproducts of a positive, national perspective.

The first European settlers came to the North American continent in search of prosperity and to escape the constraints of their homelands. Once the Colonists gained their independence, they established a republic centered around individual rights, where the government would be strong, yet not permitted to restrict the human potential. Out of this noble design, the United States became more than a haven for the persecuted; it became a nation where people were free to either prosper or to fail by their own deeds. Without a ceiling over one's head, there was no limit to the heights that could be reached and, therefore, no limit to one's aspirations.

As the word of this credo spread, the United States began receiving an influx of ambitious personality types from all over the globe, which resulted in an ever-increasing populace of goal setters and achievers. There was a strong common desire—a subconscious, uniform mindset—to achieve a better way of life. The industriousness of these immigrants and their progeny quickly transformed the United States into the world's foremost social, economic, and military power. We evolved from an upstart union of colonies into the world's entrepreneurial epicenter. The Constitution was the nidus for individual achievement, but it was the atypical psychological makeup of the immigrant populace that made the country truly unique.

This exceptional success was due to a diligence and determination that some have called the "Protestant Work Ethic," but that title does a great disservice to Catholics, Jews, Agnostics, and others who also contributed to the growth of this nation. A more appropriate title would be "American Work Ethic:" a phenomenon of human self-motivation. This country's early dreams became realities due to the concentrating of extraordinary ambitions and talents from a myriad of cultures and faiths, and, as a whole, these immigrants had positive outlooks.

Let's refrain from giving too many accolades to the USA, however, until we first examine some perspectives that significantly differ from the flag-waving one just used to characterize this industrious nation. There are other viewpoints that need to be considered. The study of America's roots would not be complete without spending some time on its indigenous residents and those who were brought here involuntarily.

As a whole, Native Americans have not experienced the prosperity of the general population. Why might that be? Over the decades, their numbers have steadily declined, while the populations of other groups have dramatically increased. Many Native Americans remain impoverished, isolated, and disenfranchised when compared to the norm, even though they have equal rights. Why haven't they achieved an equal portion of the American dream?

Early Native Americans were a proud people, respectful of their environment. They led fairly simple lives, rich in tradition and in perfect balance with nature. Their daily existence revolved around their villages, families, and spiritual beliefs. Honor, relationships, and responsibility to their tribes took precedence over material things. Could it be that they have not experienced an equal growth in prosperity because of the white man's domination, or might it be, instead, that they did not experience the American dream because they chose to retain their traditional perspectives, rather than adopt perspectives that were uncomfortable for them?

Native Americans did not immigrate to North America in pursuit of new opportunities and prosperity. This was already their homeland. Their motivations were simply framed by a perennial desire to remain secure in their accustomed way of life. They sought nothing new and they had nothing they needed to prove. To them the white man's avarice was an abomination. They were pushed aside and awarded second-class status primarily because of their unwillingness to embrace a foreign ideology.

The most significant dissimilarities between Native Americans and those who arrived on sailing ships were their perspectives. If their perspectives had been more alike, their cultures would have blended more readily. To expand on this point, let's briefly consider one more unique American subgroup: African Americans.

African Americans are another body of people who, as a whole, have not been able to equal the achievements of the white colonists and their descendants. But, before any judgment is made, one must give thought to the unique circumstance of their arrival on this continent.

Most pre-Civil War black people were brought here by force. They didn't come here with expectations of being prosperous and enjoying new freedoms; these were not among a slave's privileges. Wealth was not even a possibility. Enduring their plight, moment by moment, was the only realistic goal for these victimized human beings.

Although The Emancipation Proclamation of 1861 abolished slavery, African Americans remained inferior human beings in the eyes of many because of their long history of subservience. Newly acquired freedoms did not gain them equal status with the rest of the population, and "freedom" did not translate into "acceptance." Even if there had been no racial distinction, it is likely that former slaves would have had a difficult time emulating the same goals as other immigrants, due to their being guided by an entirely different, African American perspective that grew from their unique history.

It has only been two modern lifetimes since the American slaves were freed and granted self-determination. It's quite unfair for descendants of a goal-achieving ancestry to be judgmental of someone whose forefathers only lived a day-to-day existence, with their well-being entirely determined by others.

Definitions and perspectives are perpetuated from generation to generation, and unpleasant times make the greatest impact on an individual's personal definitions and resulting perspective. When a cluster of closely-bonded people are raised in a hostile environment, the perspectives they acquire are intertwined with a great deal of emotion, which makes those perspectives unusually tenacious.

The mindsets of parents are impressed upon their offspring, and the more isolated or segregated a group, the more intact the perspectives that are passed along. This is why, by and large, poverty breeds poverty and wealth breeds wealth. A Caucasian child from a poor family in Appalachia, whose sole source of income is cutting wood, has a smaller chance of achieving wealth than an African American child born to wealthy parents who work in Silicon Valley. Immediate influences are hugely responsible for shaping one's future. If a person, regardless of race or culture, is raised in an impoverished community where defeatist perspectives predominate, the odds of achieving a positive perspective are slim at best.

These generalizations certainly don't apply to every individual, and it must be emphasized that they have absolutely nothing to do with skin color. They do, however, have a great deal to do with cultural distinction. The effective differences between all coteries of people are entirely the result of contrasting histories and the perpetuation of ideologies through the imprinting of beliefs and perspectives on each succeeding generation. Every culture has a distinguishable, incomparable way of looking at things. An individual assimilates those perspectives, which then steer him through life.

It's impossible for you to impartially judge the thoughts and actions of other people, because your prejudice prevents you from thinking objectively. Bias is natural and unavoidable. It comes into play every time your perspective bumps into one that's dissimilar. You are partial to whatever fits into your comfort zone, and what is comfortable for you is uncomfortable for someone else. It is bias vs. bias. As you can see, a lot is at play here.

A perspective is the aspect in which something is viewed. "view" in this context is a judgment. In other words, perspective is entirely a subjective thing. It isn't right or wrong, and it's not necessarily even based on accurate facts. It's the point of reference for an individual's or group's interpretation of what is true or important: an orientation created by influences, definitions, prejudices, and intent.

Perspectives determine how one's moments are defined. They establish the parameters within which opinions are formulated, usually with minimal or no contemplation needed. They are influential, and can work for you or against you.

"Perspective" and "definition" may seem nearly synonymous, but these two words are far from identical. Whereas a definition is objective and specific, a perspective is subjective and nonspecific. There is one exception, however: a "personal definition." This variant is entirely subjective, and nearly synonymous with "perspective." A personal definition is an individual's *chosen* interpretation, a definition that arises from one's subjective reasoning.

A personal definition is an opinion, not a fact. It is the reality a person chooses to believe. The creation of a personal definition begins with a subjective analysis of the situation being studied, followed by a sometimes accurate/sometimes inaccurate conclusion that is then mentally stored under the category of "fact." Although it might be more appropriate to classify these personal definitions as "theories," they none the less constitute a huge portion of the data on which a belief system is founded. The combined effect of all your objective and personal definitions is what makes up your primary perspective.

***

If this chapter has made even the tiniest dent in the armor of your existing primary perspective, then you have the potential to make changes that will pilot you to a more peaceful state of mind. In order to release the potential that is locked inside you, you must reassess your definitions. Whenever possible, replace them with less restrictive definitions that will broaden your primary perspective, making it more adaptive and free-flowing. It's best to be open-minded and to process information as it occurs, rather than deferring to stored definitions that may be outdated or incorrect. Begin looking at everything with less bias. See if you can attain an unobstructed, 360-degree view of life.

The next chapters will expand your insight, one step at a time, to build new interpretations and to form new attitudes about everything. These changes will shed negatives and attract positives. For the first time, you will be able to rely on definitions that don't conflict with one another. Instead, they will work as a team. The net effect of these improved definitions will be a primary perspective that interprets your world more positively. This new perspective will be your fortress of strength, your guide throughout life.

In order to improve your mind's database, a mere spring cleaning will not be enough. You must get rid of the clutter. It's time to go through all your "stuff" and reduce its volume to only that which is essential. The more you can throw out, the more comfortable and efficient your new perspective will be. By streamlining your thinking, you will simplify everything.

Don't continue to emulate Congress. Every year they pass volumes of laws and regulations that add to the tens of thousands that already exist. Each legislature feels it has a duty to solve problems by adding more regulations, rather than reworking existing ones. The culling of unnecessary or ineffective laws is rarely considered, even though the burden of understanding so many dictates is overwhelming. The result is an unfathomable complexity.

You create your own mishmash of information when you continually add new definitions on top of others. Some of the definitions that your brain has stored are completely incompatible with your core beliefs, and you do not even realize it. You have stored so much information that you have forgotten all that's there, embarrassingly evident whenever you contradict yourself. Without shredding outdated data and rewriting your own laws and regulations to make them more easily understood, how can you expect anything but stalemate as you try to formulate a plan for happiness?

It's vital that you tell yourself, "My conclusions are not set in stone." If you have a sincere desire to streamline your thinking, this statement alone will initiate a more constructive mindset, improving your ability to separate truth from fiction. This is so important! Your deductions must be founded on truth, the reinforcement that keeps a positive perspective from collapsing.

5

The Collective Ego

The innate, egoistic nature of each individual insures a collective, group ego whenever individuals join together. Every coterie of people naturally deems itself "special" in one way or another. This perception results in group biases that, in turn, influence each individual.

Being distinguished by residence, affiliation, or race, whether voluntary or involuntary, puts a person in a specific box, apart from those who fit into other boxes. Each of these boxes holds individuals who have something in common, and who, by that distinction, are somewhat foreign to those with different distinctions. When groups of people feel most comfortable inside their own familiar boxes, the result is prejudice, whether realized or not.

Prejudice reduces your ability to see beyond yourself, thereby restricting the information you receive. In order to improve your reasoning, it's best to de-personalize your perceptions. This not only reduces the distortions caused by your own ego but also those caused by the various groups that have been influencing you.

Your ego prefers to believe it has virtue on its side. Those who do battle, whether it's in a war, a sporting contest, or a debate, typically see themselves as the "good guys," and their opponents as the "bad guys." Perceiving yourself as being one of the "good guys" strengthens the attachment you have with the others on your side. Not only are your thoughts and actions influenced by your group's ideology, but that influence is strengthened by the sense that you are part of something that is righteous to some degree. The beliefs born of such a bond are closed-minded to contrary opinions. When your information is restricted to only that which supports a specific doctrine, you limit your ability to see things truthfully, even if you are a forthright person.

The collective ego of a nation influences the perspectives of its individual citizens. Being raised under the influence of a US collective ego, I will use my country as an example, but similarities can be found when scrutinizing any populace, any group.

Since its inception, the United States has perceived itself as being special. The founding fathers strove to make their country the best of the best, and the motto, "In God We Trust," symbolizes the righteousness permeating their design. This noble intent, along with a history of economic and military successes, has helped form a strong sense of American pride.

When it first emerged as a new nation, the US was an upstart with everything to prove. Americans now quite comfort ably chant "U-S-A, U-S-A, U-S-A…" at events such as the Olympics, where their pride is broadcasted to the world. It's not arrogant for a country to show support for its sports teams, but it is arrogant to display pride in an overbearing manner. A propensity for many Americans to boast, rather than to show humility, has led to parts of the world perceiving all Americans as being arrogant. This label may be correct if it is the national persona being defined, but it is incorrect if used to categorize each and every citizen.

The mindset of the collective is an average of the mindsets of all its individuals. It is not necessarily the mindset of a specific individual in the group. Whereas a nation of people can be perceived as being presumptuous, an individual from that nation can be perceived as being humble. One can feel prejudice toward a certain collective, yet build strong, non-prejudiced relationships with individuals within that collective.

You have the freedom to pick and choose how you interpret your perceptions. However, repetitive exposures to the philosophies of a group can eventually make inroads into your private mindset, gradually drawing you into beliefs and actions that you would have rejected in the absence of those indoctrinations.

One of the greatest indoctrinators is the American media. One cannot watch television or read newspapers without being influenced. The news is almost always given a collective spin, sometimes obvious, sometimes disguised. It takes place through the choice of words used to relate a newsworthy event or by what is emphasized, downplayed, or hidden.

The US media gives little attention to the achievements and the prosperity of others around the world. People tend to not see very far beyond themselves anyway, and, regrettably, the media reinforces that narrow vision. This contributes to Americans believing that they are exceptional, which, to a degree, is more illusion than fact. Whether through indoctrinations, lack of information, or from our own natural sense of pride, Americans have acquired an inflated collective ego. This is a dangerous thing to have, because it can cause us to naively believe that we are infallible and that our perspectives are sound.

It's sobering for me to realize that I am part of that collective ego, and that most of my beliefs are not my own. My base ideologies were pretty much manufactured by others, and I have had very little to say about it. I know my belief system would be entirely different had I grown up in China or Afghanistan. If a person's ideology depends on where and how he is raised, then any man fighting against another, no matter what the circumstances, is no different than one man against his brother, or even against himself. All humans are essentially interconnected; differing perspectives are what make us think and act differently.

To become your own person, rather than one whose thoughts are determined by others, you need to free yourself from the collective ego, those who have been indoctrinated and manipulated all their lives to behave in a unified, habitual fashion. You don't have to remain ensconced in the beliefs of others. You can choose a better perspective.

Perspectives range from the collective view of the entire world populace, through the countless societal subgroups, and ending with the perspectives of single individuals. As you have read, an ego (the self as distinguished from others) can elect to either stand alone or join a group ego. Therefore, a person isn't restricted to a single point of view, and a perspective will vary according to where the mind has anchored itself at any given moment. This range of perceptions is like boxes of varying sizes that are able to nest, one within the other, such as those shown in the following diagram:

Perspective Options

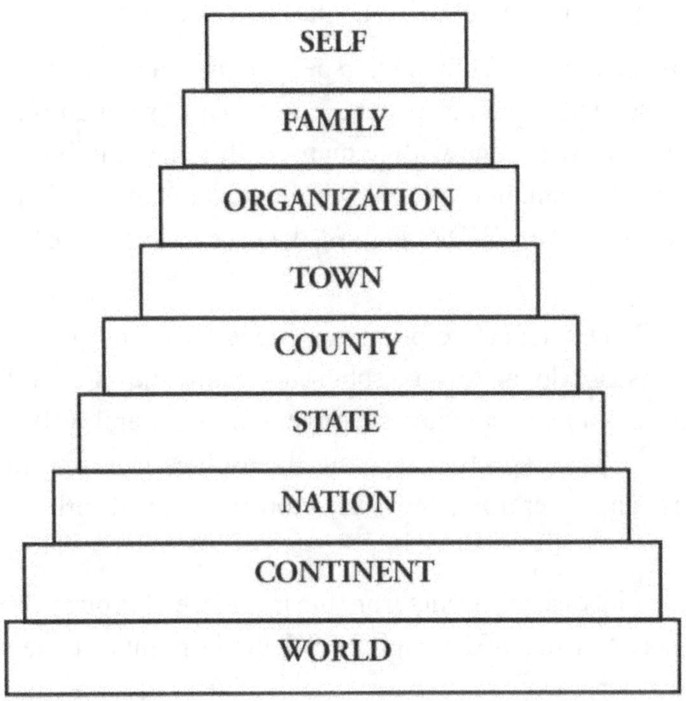

Any singular point of view encompasses all those that are less broad, just as any one of these individual boxes holds all smaller boxes within it. I am currently a resident of Michigan, and thus can adopt the general perspective of millions of Michiganders. That STATE box includes the consecutively smaller boxes, COUNTY, TOWN, ORGANIZATION, FAMILY, and SELF.

When I want to see things from a broader perspective, I can choose to think of myself as an American, rather than a Michigander. Although that NATION box is only one box larger than the STATE box, it includes forty-nine additional states, and every one of those state's smaller boxes as well.

An individual has all perspectives available, because the SELF box can fit within any other box. An individual has the option to join any other group or he can remain independent. The individual always remains an individual, but depending on which box he chooses to occupy, his point of reference either narrows or expands.

When selecting a WORLD perspective, a mind joins the blending of every possible human perspective, since that box contains all others. This point of view is "one with humanity." It's the only box without a competitor. All smaller boxes within it contain prejudices and competing egos. The WORLD box does not have an ego needing nourishment.

A WORLD perspective promotes cooperation and understanding, because it is not loyal to any subgroup. Someone with a WORLD perspective has a personal interest in everyone's general welfare. Those who choose this perspective separate themselves from the individual collectives, and, therefore, they are more able to absorb the bigger picture.

Most social discord occurs from the influence of group perspectives that fall between the SELF and the WORLD points of view. These intermediary boxes are where perspectives become noisy and dysfunctional by the fragmenting of what otherwise might be an unambiguous world. Divergent opinions and alliances undermine common sense, inevitably leading to conflict.

The priorities of most people are obviously misplaced, since few are at peace with life. You can learn from them, but you don't want to be like them. Keep this in mind: Most of what others believe is the result of prejudiced interpretations, not the result of facts. Happiness will elude you if you allow so many extraneous concerns into your mind that you end up having no clear purpose. It's equally self-defeating to allow a too-restrictive point of view to prevail, because then you shrink your options and miss out on many opportunities. To best utilize life's resources, you must think independently, yet openly.

By reducing your attachment to intermediate alliances, your emotional stability will improve. But try as you might, you will never be a completely passive observer of the collective ego, since everyone that you know plays a part in it, and it has already made a permanent impact on you. What you can do is limit its negative effects by thinking as independently as possible.

Only the SELF or WORLD perspective should be used when making your personal definitions. Try to disengage yourself from all those perspectives in between. You need a tightly focused SELF perspective as your inner, everyday guide. Then, when you need to constructively relate to the bigger picture, switch to a WORLD perspective. The intermediate perspectives should be passed over. They amplify prejudice and obscure truth. Having a few prejudices can't be avoided—it goes with being a feeling person—but those definitions should be derived from your own perceptions, not from the myopic vision of the masses.

6

The Ultimate Perspective

Though this journey began in darkness, the sun is beginning to rise. You are now ready to venture ahead, although you are not entirely sure of your destination, let alone the route you must take. Many a great day begins blanketed in light fog, so don't be concerned if you are still having difficulty seeing where you are going. The mist will soon dissipate, and your way will become crystal clear. The morning air is fresh and invigorating, you are inspired, and today is filled with promise. Your first steps begin...

Few realize the limitations that outdated perspectives place on them. Antiquated interpretations are anchors that weigh against revelation. Your goal is to break down the perspective walls that are imprisoning you before they become your tomb. To accomplish this, you must alter the harmful interpretations that you've assigned to many of your perceptions. The skill to do this has always been with you, but your acceptance of these interpretations has suppressed that ability.

In order to gain, then maintain, a better perspective, you must become an independent thinker, re-exploring the world around you to discover what is, not what you have assumed, so that you untether your uniqueness. Whatever your resources—material, physical or intellectual—and regardless of your mind's present state, you can reach a higher plane. Do not underestimate your potential, for inside you resides the nobility and spirit of the amazing human intellect. Don't worry if you do not yet feel strong. If your inner strength has been concealed, it's about to be coaxed out of hiding.

Hopefully, the previous chapters have initiated the re-evaluation of your belief system. They have been a purposeful manipulation, just as others have manipulated you throughout your life. The uniqueness of this manipulation, however, is that you are not being coerced into adopting someone else's prejudices; you are being coached to think for yourself. It's time to develop a more discerning eye. It's time to see the good in the bad and the bad in the good, and to take that insight and develop a perspective that is your own—not the author's, not your mother's, not your teachers', and certainly not that of any collective ego.

As you continue reading, consider this writing as it was meant to be: an instrument rather than a bible. Explore its messages, and then pay attention to the dialogue that takes place within you. Pause for a moment during your personal insights and write them down. Turn this book into a diary of your own discoveries. Prepare yourself to eventually leave these pages behind, and take with you an understanding of life that is your own creation.

Your current perspective is already different from when you first began to read *The Changeover*. It has changed automatically, moment to moment. Perspectives are always in a state of adaptation and refinement, because a brain continuously catalogs new facts. But, from this point on, more than an automatic processing will be needed. Thoughtfully consider what you read next. Take your time. Look to gain wisdom, and allow yourself to be transformed by new realizations.

This moment is the only one in which you are living. Make it the one that makes all your upcoming moments better. Don't postpone your happiness, for life is way too short. As you come up with ideas that will make things better, implement them. If you have a history of procrastination, don't let this be one of those times. Make the commitment to live a life founded on truth. Make it a priority! Most importantly, dedicate yourself to the discovery of positive truths that will result in a more positive perspective.

***

Every now and then, when the sun breaks through the clouds after a rainstorm, our senses are rewarded with a magnificent rainbow. How wonderful to view something so incredible and in such contrast to a darkened sky!

Rainbows are among the most positive and satisfying of all nature's works. A rainbow is simple truth. It is purity, unspoiled by man. Rainbows are uncomplicated, offering nothing more than what we see. They are universally appreciated and loved.

Rainbows inspire many feelings. Here are a few words and phrases that come to mind when I envision a rainbow:

Relaxation

Appreciation

Peace

Reward

Hope

Healing

Love

Beauty

Understanding

Encouragement

Time to pause

Catch a breath

Time to reflect

Better things ahead

Now close your eyes and imagine your own rainbow, one arching majestically overhead, then take a minute to contemplate how it makes you feel and what thoughts or words it inspires...........................

....

You may find it hard to believe, but it's possible to feel this way most of the time!

The previous chapters dealt primarily with understanding your belief system. In summary, almost everything that comprises the way you think is the result of indoctrinations, biased opinions, and pure chance circumstance. You have a mind that determines how those beliefs are expressed, but up until now you have been a fabrication, you have not been entirely your own creation. This has resulted in a significant amount of subconscious turmoil because your mind has had difficulty sorting out what it is that you really do believe. As a result, you have experienced many sunny days and many rainy days, but not nearly enough rainbows. You deserve more of them. You are about to free yourself from that phase of your life and become self-made. You are about to cast off the beliefs of others and become your own person for the very first time. You will accomplish this changeover by building a new belief system that will result in an *Ultimate Perspective*.

You are not stuck with what you have become. You can escape your bindings, discover a new and better life, and become the person you've always wished to be, all by way of perspective. There are three perspectives that we will address: an *individual perspective*, a *primary perspective*, and an *Ultimate Perspective*.

Individual Perspective: Your perspective on any one of thousands of topics; your "take" on a singular subject or experience.

Primary Perspective: Your main outlook on life; the combined result of all your individual perspectives.

Ultimate Perspective: A positive primary perspective; an inspired outlook that produces a healthy mind.

By now you should have a pretty good understanding of what is an *individual perspective*. It's what you are referring to when you say things like, "Let's put this into proper perspective," or "My perspective on this is...," or "We need to look at this situation from another perspective." An individual perspective is an independent, specific point of view.

Because each individual perspective has its own, unique origin, inconsistencies permeate your thinking. Should you assume that there is continuity in your individual perspectives—a seamless theme that molds all of your opinions—all you have to do to realize "it ain't so" is scan your thoughts for contradictions. For example, you might think all insects are creepy yet go outside and exclaim, "What an awesome butterfly!" More profound are the perspective variations you will find regarding other humans. You look at your own race differently than you do another, and you regard your neighbors differently than you do your family.

How you generally feel about your world, therefore how you direct your entire thinking process, depends on the combined effect of your individual perspectives. This net compilation is your *primary perspective*. A primary perspective is not so much a specific point of view as it is the emotional summary of all individual perspectives that form it. This outcome is responsible for a general attitude that is positive, negative, or indifferent. If twenty percent of your individual perspectives involve pleasant perceptions, and eighty percent unpleasant ones, your primary perspective is going to be predominantly negative. There will be some good moments in your life, but most of the time you won't be happy. On the other hand, if twenty percent of your individual perspectives engender negative feelings but the larger eighty percent augment your happiness, then your primary perspective will affect you like a rainbow, coloring your life with predominantly good perceptions.

Lasting contentment results when one achieves an Ultimate Perspective, which is a *positive* primary perspective generated by the acquisition of a predominance of positive individual perspectives. An Ultimate Perspective is conditional on your being pleased with the majority of what you discern. It can't materialize if negatives permeate your individual perspectives.

An Ultimate Perspective is not unlike a rainbow, in that it is a phenomenon that precipitates soothing sensory perceptions. The attainment of such a primary perspective has a profound effect on one's psyche. When the summation of all one's perceptions provides a net, positive attitude, the result is authentic happiness.

It's difficult to find words to properly describe the concept of a "primary perspective," a subconscious manifestation that is entirely responsible for how you generally feel. It arises from revelations more than from measured assessments, but whereas most recognizable revelations are the result of dramatic events, your primary perspective is the end product of the routine workings of your mind. A primary perspective is influential. It expresses itself as subtle seasoning for all your thoughts, flavoring your perceptions rather than creating them.

A primary perspective is as expansive as a perspective can be. Instead of being a point of view, it is an infinite view. It is determined by your state of mind, which in turn is determined by how you interpret your state of affairs. Your primary perspective depends on how your personal definitions affect you and how much that *general* feeling influences your *general* thinking. With the word "general" utilized to describe this state of mind and its related feelings, it may sound as though this perspective is only of moderate importance, but your *general attitude* is your guiding life force. That attitude can push you in any number of directions, and it ultimately determines your *general* well-being, which is a matter of *specific* importance!

Everyone has a primary perspective. It is responsible for one's energy, outlook, awareness, mindset, and expectancy of things to come. It is not the soul expressed; it is the soul felt. A primary perspective influences one's life experience more than anything else because it dictates how life is interpreted.

Your body is a miraculous creation, and when the role of every internal organ is scrutinized, the end product makes sense. We readily recognize the importance of each of our separate parts, and when those parts are properly interconnected, those organs form an entity that is special.

Your individual perspectives can be thought of as being your individual organs, and your primary perspective as being the result of connecting those parts. Your primary perspective is to your individual definitions and interpretations what your soul is to your body's cells and neurons. A primary perspective is a powerful, omniscient presence.

The Genesis of Perspectives:

1. Personal experience and opinion > > >>>>Personal Definition
2. Related personal definitions > > > > >>>Individual Perspective
3. Combined individual perspectives > > > Primary Perspective

Nothing makes more of an impact than a new experience. When you were an infant, every experience was new, and each new stimulus received your full attention. Initially, you had no opinions to influence your perceptions, but it didn't take long before your first personal definitions were formed. They were likely related to your basic needs, such as your need for nourishment. A couple of those initial definitions were *When I'm hungry—that's bad,* and *When I'm being fed—that's good.*

In those early moments, every event was significant to your newly functioning mind, and each experience required an interpretation. As your intelligence grew, so did the number of definitions and their related individual perspectives. Eventually, all that information was polled, a consensus determined, and *voilá*, you formed a primary perspective. At last, order sprang from chaos, taking control of the many separate perspectives, eliminating their anarchy, and establishing a set of rules for processing all new information.

Everyone lives in a private universe, each with a unique design. Some look like ghettos, others like well-kept gardens. Your universe is the result of all input, all thought. The more knowledge you have and the more you open up to the positives that life has to offer, the bigger and better your universe becomes. The less information you process, and the more negative your definitions, the more your universe contracts.

Your universe is conjoined with your primary perspective. You can't change one without affecting the other. To access new bountiful worlds, you must attain a positive attitude, an Ultimate Perspective. If you aren't already a positive person, you can become more authentically positive by only one of two ways:

1) You can directly implement an Ultimate Perspective—an honest belief that life is predominantly positive—which will then do the work of redefining negative images for you.

2) You can make new, more positive interpretations of the facts responsible for your individual perspectives, so that they then automatically provide you with an Ultimate Perspective.

If you are exceptionally disciplined, the first option will bring about the quickest improvement. This is what motivational writers and speakers try to elicit: instant change. But, immediately casting off an established, negative primary perspective takes more skill than what most people have. To establish an Ultimate Perspective at the onset requires exceptional faith and willpower, and if that perspective isn't thoroughly believed, it will break down when attacked by new negatives.

The second method does not provide instant change, but building a perspective from the ground up is how any determined individual can attain results that are both predictable and durable. Adjusting one's definitions provides a perspective that doesn't have to rely on willpower or faith, because the changeover is automatic.

What you are seeking is an improved emotional state. As mentioned earlier, this is a personal issue. The logic you will call upon to gain a positive outlook on life may be the opposite of what someone else would use. There are no standard ingredients, and there is no specific recipe to follow. Only your definitions and your feelings count. Logic sets this process in motion, but feelings are what need to be satisfied, since good feelings are what you are seeking. Perfection may not be the result, but perfection should be your target. When a realization begins to work for you, take it as far as you can. Always go forward, never backward. Your ultimate goal is to reach a point where you feel and believe that life is good.

A perspective is a point of view, an interpretation. It is influenced by facts, assumptions, and emotions. If you are surrounded by unhappiness, and you allow only negative people to influence you, you will have a negative primary perspective. In order to feel good, you must perceive the moment as being good. You can't be happy, regardless of the positives that surround you, if you perceive the moment as unpleasant. You can tell yourself, *I'm going to think positively today*, but unless you actually believe that something positive is happening, the positive attitude that you put on is nothing more than self-deceit. Without a primary perspective that honestly believes that positives significantly outnumber negatives, a positive attitude cannot continue day after day.

You can become inherently happy, but only through honesty, not deceit. You can't improve your attitude by pretending to feel good. A genuinely positive perspective is founded on positive truths. The next chapters will teach you how to find them. They surround you, and they are plentiful. Your job will be to discover the positive side of every situation. You will use your positive discoveries to build an invulnerable fortress that will become your Ultimate Perspective. It's not enough to presume or to take someone's word that these positives exist; you must find them yourself so that you will have confidence in their validity.

You were previously offered an analogy of nesting boxes, from the smallest to the largest. They represented various levels of perspective that are available to you. However, each individual box contains its own nesting perspectives that also come in varying sizes and complexities, ranging from very narrow to extremely broad. It's possible to have a separate, distinct perspective regarding a tiny bit of data, or one that encompass an entire library of information.

Your general happiness is determined by the net effect of all of your individual perspectives. This "primary perspective" takes in your entire view of life and all it entails. It's made up of both positive and negative definitions. When life seems dissatisfying, it's because you perceive the negatives to be outweighing the positives. In order for a primary perspective to help you feel good, it must predominantly consist of interpretations that are positive and constructive to the outlook you want to have.

An individual perspective is relatively insignificant by itself. It doesn't have the power to defeat the stronger, primary perspective. For example, if you have a general perspective that's dominated by the interpretation, "the pursuit of happiness is futile," an individual perspective based on the definition, "chocolate is awesome," won't have sufficient positive weight to override your primary, negative outlook. It would take the addition of many positive individual perspectives to dent such an attitude. That's why a birthday or a holiday cannot defeat a state of depression.

A moment of positives, no matter how outstanding, is never enough to conquer a negative outlook. When someone is counting on a single event to improve how they feel, and it doesn't happen, the depression often becomes even more severe. However, an individual perspective multiplied a thousand-fold is a profound force, one that demands that a primary perspective pay attention. A thousand positive perceptions can undo a depressed state of mind.

What perspective best fits your goals? If you are ambitious and want to live life to the max, you'll need a perspective that contains some angst as well as positive energy; you needn't be perfectly content. If your goal is to achieve maximum peace and contentment, then an angst-free outlook is what you should seek. If you can't accept the world as it is, and plan to do something about it, your new perspective will need to retain an edge of negativity.

What outlook is the best match for your soul? Some perspectives occur more naturally than others. You have the option to expand on what's been comfortable for you, or you can break new ground. The path of least resistance usually indicates your most compatible option.

What is realistic to accomplish? There are no limits, as long as your perspective is one that you can honestly support. Remember, you have to believe in it; it can't be a charade. Desire will become fact if you believe what you are doing is important enough to carry the task to completion.

To determine what needs to be done, begin with a list of words and phrases that describe how you would like to feel. Achieving a perspective that can be defined by those words will satisfy your heartfelt needs. Those words will be the essence of the Ultimate Perspective that you'll create.

The beat of an improved perspective is resonating inside you. Soon it will become a rhythm that will replace your old outlook. Until that is accomplished, however, you may experience your own "Battle of Perspectives." Mixing a well-intentioned, but embryonic, Ultimate Perspective with existing, negative interpretations is bound to bring conflict at times, but as negative perceptions are converted into positive ones, a solid Ultimate Perspective will eventually dominate.

Strive to eliminate those definitions that don't belong anymore, and capture a few rainbows to augment the positives already in your database. You'll find that as your Ultimate Perspective strengthens, it will begin casting your individual perspectives in the most beneficial light possible without your having to make conscious changes. As you become more able to deal positively with adversity whenever it presents itself, your positive energy will grow even stronger, and that will preclude you from slipping back into negativity, as so frequently happens when an ambition must stand the test of time.

I hope you are becoming comfortable with the concept of a "primary perspective." Highlight the word, "perspective," in your awareness. Make it a common part of your inner dialogue, and use the word in your communications with family and friends. The more you use it, the better you'll understand it. The more comfortable the concept becomes, the more quickly you'll reach your goal. Whenever you feel an emotion, whenever you interpret information, and whenever you simply awaken to the moment, think *PERSPECTIVE*. There is nothing more significant, for it is the major determinant for every realization and emotion that you have.

Ultimate Perspective Key #1:

THE KEY TO MENTAL WELL-BEING

IS THE ACHIEVEMENT OF A

POSITIVE PRIMARY PERSPECTIVE.

7

A Pair of Threes

In grade school you were taught the "Three Rs." Here are three more to master: **RECOGNITION**, **REALIZATION**, and **RETENTION**.

RECOGNITION (identifying interpretations harmful to your dream):

This changeover is all about enlightenment. Don't assume that your current vision is unclouded by other peoples' prejudices or egos. Instead of continuing to accept their manipulations, take charge. Enter each new situation with open eyes. Be aware and beware. Decide what information is beneficial to you, and what is not worthy of your time. Don't accept everything that you hear at face value; search out the truth.

REALIZATION (your dream coming true): By utilizing positive truths, build a dominating, positive perspective that meets your goal of making the most of each day. Celebrate your independence. Enjoy the beauty in life, and appreciate things never before appreciated. Be the person you wish to be by living a life of value. Experience a more peaceful mind.

RETENTION (living your dream): Your mental state is influenced by each new experience. Resist being the easy prey of manipulators who act in their own interests. Don't permit the outside world to contaminate your improved perspective. It's your creation, and you are the one who controls its composition. Don't allow the return of negative thinking! When you fall down, recover. When you fatigue, re-energize. When you are pushed aside, bounce back. Continue to support your positive inclination.

In revamping your belief system, there may be a time when you'll be able to consider a fact and immediately give it a constructive definition, but in the beginning, you'll have to be careful not to form opinions too quickly, especially when they pertain to important matters. Until a significant amount of reprogramming has been completed, your perspective can't be trusted to help you make the best interpretations.

Remember, your current perspective is corrupt. You might assume that you know what you're doing, and you may feel good about your progress thus far, but until you have either redefined or eliminated some of the more influential negatives in your current perspective, those negatives will be barriers to your goal.

It's unwise to begin a construction project without first establishing an uncompromised building site. I learned this the hard way. I once owned a small, lakeside cottage which I decided to convert into a year-round home. I wanted the construction to go as quickly as possible, and my goal was to keep the cost down. I drew the plans myself and contracted with a local builder to achieve the results that I desired, utilizing as much of the original structure as possible. After reducing half the old building to rubble, reinforcing the antiquated foundation, connecting new plumbing and electric lines to the original service, and joining new walls and roof to the old, the home ended up being an architectural masterpiece, just as I had envisioned.

Although…would you believe that our contractor was faced with so many unforeseen problems that it took twice as long as estimated to complete the project? Should I admit that the cost ended up being more than it would have been had I leveled the old place and built a new home from scratch? Shall I swallow my pride and confess that the basement filled with water every spring—just as it did before the home was remodeled—and I had to deal with a leaky roof and other problems more typical of an older home than one newly built? Overlaying new construction on top of a questionable foundation proved to be a big mistake. The same holds true when building a perspective.

Your brain is a computer. It's made up of cells rather than microchips, but it is, nonetheless, a computer. Once entered into the hard drive, all data, such as your experiences and your definitions, become permanently stored and remain in their original state unless revised or deleted. This data is responsible for your conscious interpretations, and also the subconscious, automatic responses that are frequently elicited by new stimuli. Your computer determines whether to initiate a thought process, a physical reaction, or a flowing of emotions. Your programming can automatically take you up or down. It can reinforce your perspective—whether healthy or unhealthy—or create a new one.

When information is fed into this computer, it is sorted, catalogued, and put into folders containing similar input. Your brain uses this data to direct your life, and to interpret new information that's then also stored. Unless existing files are intentionally altered, nothing ever changes, with interpretations and the way the computer automatically responds to new stimuli remaining as dated as its programming.

There's a limit to the volume of data a computer can handle. As disk space fills up, a computer becomes less efficient. When this happens, the only way that disk space can be regained is to retire programs and files that are nonproductive.

By cleaning up your mental computer, it's possible to improve every aspect of brain performance, including your perspective. Many of your perceived inadequacies are simply the result of data disarray rather than faulty hardware. As you follow the steps to creating a better primary perspective, you'll become more clear-headed, your memory will improve, you'll be able to process information more quickly, and your senses will heighten. Your mind will be a far better machine once it has been freed from years of accumulated clutter.

To improve upon your programming, you must first investigate your database, and then make corrections to the errors you find. Be prepared to modify many of the opinions you currently hold. As I have repeatedly suggested, don't cling blindly to old beliefs. Don't let them own you!

You've been imprisoned by a lifetime of harmful assumptions that need to be discarded. Know that you can free yourself. Believe that better feelings are attainable. Enter this process with a positive expectation, and enjoy the quest. Strive to accentuate what is right in the world. Envision alpine meadows rather than graveyards.

***

Next are some visualizations that will help clarify what you need to do. Allow me to introduce you to three faces, the second of this chapter's "Pair of Threes:"

FACE #1

Stored Information

(before reprogramming)

Traditional mental health counseling is centered on rooting out and then resolving the dominant negatives in a mental program. It's rationalized that by dealing effectively with the major items that are causing distress, everything else will then begin to fall into place. This theory assumes that there are specific causative factors responsible for an inability to cope, and that if these are eliminated, balance will be restored or, better yet, the scale will tip toward a positive state of mind.

Working toward this goal certainly helps—and for a simple mind it can be the simple cure—but, our times and minds are not as simple as they once were. Even positively-inclined people find it difficult to cope with the sheer volume of material circulating in their craniums these days. Alleviating the major aggravators can help one to feel better for a while, but achieving a partial fix is no different than removing only a portion of a cancerous growth. A malignancy can't be cured this way. At best, its progress can be decelerated. It's no wonder that some people spend years in counseling without seeming to get anywhere. How can troubled souls ever expect to get a handle on all their stress makers when fighting any one of them can be a full-time battle? And, what about those problems that have yet to be addressed? What about the new stresses that keep piling on? It is understandable why depression has become an epidemic.

Common depression is emotional fatigue that occurs when one repeatedly fails to gain a positive edge. To feel good a person has to experience more positives than negatives, and perceive that he has a degree of control. But one does not have to experience a complete shutdown to feel that life is disappointing. A mediocre state can also be perceived as unacceptable. Whenever one stops putting energy into tipping the scale toward the positive, the best that can happen is an averaging-out of feelings: a neutral existence we call "the blahs." In a society where achievement is a way of life, feeling neutral is a negative. There is no happy medium for an achiever.

If you believe that in order to be appreciated, a moment must be a peak among the valleys, and if taking care of business requires so much of your time that those high points are few and far between, then you are living under too much stress. FACE #1 portrays this state of mind.

If each person is the center of his universe, imagine how many universes there must be! If your universe is only one among billions of others, could it be that you are not really the center of anything? What do you think would happen to your perspective if you began looking at everything as if you were not important at all?

In relation to all who have ever existed, you are only a petal amid acres of flowers. Textbooks have preserved the accomplishments of a few outstanding people, like Aristotle, Plato, Einstein, and Beethoven, because their talents were exceptional, and because, relatively speaking, they are our contemporaries. However, most exceptional people from the past have been forgotten. Among these: the first person to master riding upon a horse's back; the man or woman who invented the wheel; the first to create symbols that represent words. Even the greatest accomplishments fade with time. What are the odds that people will know the names Oprah Winfrey or Bill Gates ten thousand years from now? How significant does that make you?

A few generations from now, you and I will be no more important to those living than the soil we've become. No matter what heights of accomplishment we reach today, time will eventually erase all memory of our mortal existence. Our practical relevance is solely to the lives we directly affect during our lifetime. Therefore, any significance we are to the world primarily exists *now*, and our ambitions should be efficiently directed toward what can be readily touched *now*. Attempting to create a legacy for the purpose of future recognition is a folly. *Now* is the only time you can experience the positive rewards that result from your accomplishments. *Now* is definitely "where it's at."

Giving unrealistic importance to your achievements only adds stress by making you believe that you have to hurry to make a difference or accomplish something special. Why spend your time pursuing things that, in truth, bring daily frustration, rather than satisfaction? Your priorities need to be on the things that are meaningful and relevant to your everyday life. This is where you find rainbows.

Even if you have an extraordinary talent, such as the ability to motivate others, and thereby reach beyond your immediate sphere of influence, it's wise to put some of your endeavors on hold until your head is on straight. You'll be able to raise the bar even higher once you've accomplished your changeover. The reprogramming of your perspective is not the time to feed your ego, especially when that ego may be one of your worst enemies. First establish a better perspective, and then continue with your ambitions. By doing this you will ultimately achieve more.

For the time being, direct your efforts toward the things that are nearby and that best define the moment. Reduce or eliminate any emphasis you have been placing on goals or on how you are perceived by others.

RECOGNITION: You must determine what's truly important to you.

No opinion is factually less or more meaningful than another. Everything is relevant to the specific needs and desires of the individual. One person's first ride in an expensive sports car might be no more thrilling than another person's first ride in a dugout canoe. How an experience is defined depends on how it compares with other experiences that one has had. You can't know how yours compare to those of anyone else, because we each perceive things uniquely.

Happiness isn't just a privilege for the rich. Everyone can afford good feelings. A third world person can enjoy his electronic-free day as much as you do with your computer, Smart TV, and cell phone. True personal wealth is a matter of perspective, not dollars. What do you require to be truly happy? Are your ambitions inspiring you, or are they causing frustration? What is your definition of "wealth?"

Spiritual prosperity is easiest to achieve when life is uncomplicated. The less importance placed on specific items or special events, and the more attention that's given to the common things, the better off you are. Possessions and special occasions can contribute to your happiness, but they shouldn't be considered prerequisites. Joy is more readily attainable when you begin living for the moment, and thereby open yourself to steady, good vibrations.

RECOGNITION: Happiness might not be found where you've been looking.

Today is your only reality. The past and future are merely images. However, your mind has the ability to give these images the same status as present events. When such thoughts interfere with your appreciation for the moment, true reality becomes shamefully devalued. It's the living moment that can be utilized, not projections or dead issues. Being overly concerned with anything other than the present is futile. Sure, there are memories that revive good feelings, and it's smart to set things in motion so that when a date in the future becomes the present, that moment is the best it can be, but it's a terrible waste of time to chronically close one's eyes to the moment, and replace it with something that isn't real. If you are focused on the moment and that moment is enjoyable, the past and the future are irrelevant, and negative stress ceases to exist. If your "now" is good, who cares what used to be or what might be? Mental gymnastics into the past or future squander your precious time. Even if such thoughts help improve how you feel now, you must exercise care, for if you spend too much time on either side of reality, you might as well not exist at all.

RECOGNITION: The past and the future do not preclude you from utilizing today's positive harvest.

***

Thus far you have been directed to:

1) Prioritize your immediate world.
2) Open your mind to new information and new perspectives.
3) Alter detrimental labels and prejudices by incorporating new definitions.
4) Reconsider what makes you happy, and prepare to find contentment in new ways.
5) Reduce mental journeys into the past and future, reserving such travels for positive reasons only.
6) Place most of your energy into developing appreciation for things that are happening *now*.

Instead of living with fate, you are going to take control. It's time to choose your own definitions and decide how you will respond to them. Most of your perceived negatives are negative interpretations, and thus you have the ability to undo them. They exist solely in your mind, even though they may be formed out of substance. They would fade away if you would let them.

FACE #2

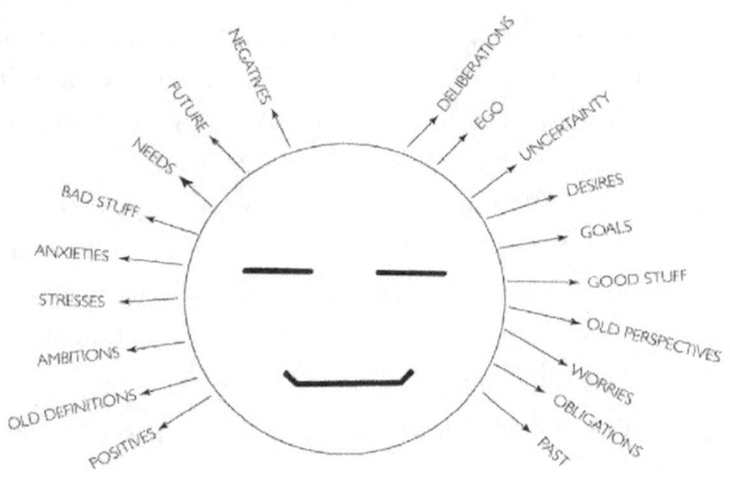

Information cleared

(a fresh beginning)

You can experience a FACE #2 with sedatives, hypnosis, or a lobotomy. But the best way is to purge all stress-causing perceptions. Note that I did not solely address *negative* perceptions. That's because even good perceptions can cause stress, and the more stress you can clear out of your mind the easier it will be to restock it with the best possible interpretations.

Before continuing further, please take a few seconds to examine the FACE #1 illustration once again……

Might that be your face? I know it was the image my mirror revealed a few years ago. It wasn't a happy face. I still can't look at FACE #1 without reliving the tension it represents. No matter how many times I see it, I become unsettled by the ghost of what I used to be, and I take it as a warning of what I could again become.

It can be a humbling experience to acknowledge the accumulation of self-defeating perspectives (a little stressful). You may feel the urge to rid yourself of negative perceptions but lack the confidence to begin tackling a project of such magnitude (more stress). Knowing that forging a solution is so imperative to your happiness, you might worry about what will happen if you are not successful turning things around (a lot more stress).

If you have these concerns, then reading this book has added at least three more stresses to your already-overcrowded skull, and they entered without anything changing in your life except the reading of someone else's words. Do you see how easy it is to acquire a negative mindset? A negative state can creep in without any specific negative being apparent.

But here's some outstanding news: You can just as easily melt away a negative mindset. You don't have to be an intellectual prodigy in order to clear your mind. In fact, it's best to hardly think about it at all. To achieve the fresh beginning depicted in FACE #2 you only need to relax your thoughts, initiating feelings of peace, rather than spotlighting your anxieties. Your mind will begin to clear once it recognizes this is what you've decided to do.

In the previous chapter, I listed words and phrases that came to mind when I envisioned rainbows. This time I'll list a few words that could relate to FACE #2:

Daylight

Openness

Relaxation

Positive

Welcoming

Peaceful

Refreshed

Acceptance

Opening Up

Receptive to Change

Enlightenment

Weight Removed

Freedom

What words would you use? How would you describe what you would feel if your stresses instantly disappeared, and you had the opportunity to begin anew? Write those words down, the more the better. If you would rather not take the time right now, at least take a short break from your reading and imagine having a frame of mind where your thoughts are uncomplicated. Think back to that alpine meadow that you previously envisioned. Visualize yourself being at peace..

....

A negative state of mind can be tenacious and so deeply ingrained that it resists being put aside, but there's no question that you have the ability to escape one—*you just did it*! If you were able to create a list of positive words or a mental picture absent of the stresses that have been on your mind, then you were successful in purging stressful input. It's that easy! Negative perceptions went away when you envisioned a positive state of being. Sure, stresses will gradually creep back in, since you did not redefine those elements, but for a while at least, they ceased to exist. The words that you wrote down or the vision that you were able to conjure cannot coexist with definitions that need changing. You can't have positive thoughts without simultaneously setting aside negative feelings.

Clearing your mind creates a vacuum, and you know what happens when a vacuum exists…things are drawn to it. Your job is to be critical of what tries to re-enter; you don't want purged negatives to return. Interrupt a negative thought as soon as you become aware of its attempt to infect you once again. Do your best to redefine it then and there, so that you can sustain your improved attitude.

FACE #3

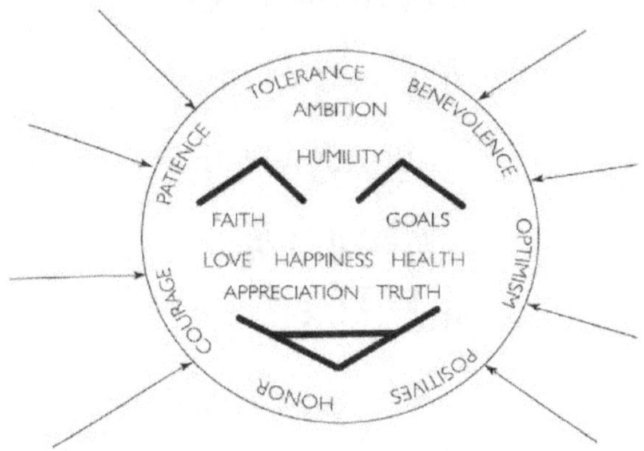

Reprogrammed

(improved stored information)

After doing your best to clear your mind, it needs to refill with definitions that will energize you and improve upon your old design, as shown in FACE #3. If it's impossible to feel both positive and negative at the same time, then it's logical that focusing on positive images will nudge you toward a positive mindset.

As you begin making definitions that are more constructive than those you have used in the past, you'll fuel a positive change and your stress will be reduced. Defining things more positively is so amazingly cool, because with the introduction of each positive redefinition, not only is a negative destroyed, but also as negatives disappear, new positives come out of the woodwork. The process then accelerates.

Become more simpleminded. There are times when this is a good thing, especially if that state correlates to an ability to function optimally in a world rife with stress and turmoil. A mind that has some breathing room can accommodate new goals, and is better at handling unexpected difficulties without them causing a stress blow-out. The "simple mind" I am describing has the following attributes:

Uncomplicated

Fundamental

Unrestricted

Unconditional

Receptive

Understandable

However, the words "foolish," "ignorant," dimwitted," and "naive" can also be used to describe a simpleminded state. When there are several definitions available, the precise meaning of a word depends on the intent of the user. When you are redefining a perception, and there are several possible definitions available—each correct, yet different— you have the option of selecting the definition that you believe is most appropriate. In the next chapter you will discover how to select better definitions for your perceptions; you will learn how to make truthful interpretations that move you toward your changeover goal of achieving an Ultimate Perspective.

8
Capturing Rainbows

Life is unpredictable and ever-changing. This volatility is tolerable because there's usually an averaging of the "highs" and the "lows." There are some individuals who seem to be fated with disproportionate shares of either positives or negatives, but when one examines the entire spectrum of life, balance exists. There is birth and death, Yin and Yang, ebb and flow, good and evil, darkness and light, pain and pleasure, storm and rainbow.

The law of averages tells us that when a person flips a coin, half the time it will land as "heads," and half the time the result will be "tails." Engineers have been able to fabricate a machine that can repeatedly flip a coin so precisely that the coin lands with the same side up each time, but a human's coin toss is variable, thus making the result unpredictable. However, a human toss can result in "heads" every time if one uses a coin that has a head stamped on both sides. Humans have the ability to do such manipulations to tip the odds in their favor, making it possible to guarantee an outcome that normally would be determined solely by chance. A two-headed coin overrides fate, and, even though using one is a manipulation, the result is fact.

You can choose to wait for the occasional rainbow—your life will experience a few of them—but wouldn't it be better if you could capture one, so that it could be viewed whenever you wanted without first having to weather a storm? You have that ability. The way to capture a rainbow is to create a positive personal definition that will guarantee an enriched perspective: your own two-headed coin. An improved reality can be constructed out of the existing facts, whatever they may be, through the manipulation of your personal definitions.

Ultimate Perspective Key #2:

THE KEY TO A POSITIVE PERSPECTIVE IS CREATING POSITIVE PERSONAL DEFINITIONS.

A dictionary definition is a factual description of a word's meaning. Synonyms are usually included to help clarify the description. As I previously described regarding the definition of "simpleminded," sometimes a word has more than one possible meaning, in which case the synonyms can vary greatly. When there are multiple definitions and synonyms available, the correct interpretation of a word can only be made by hearing or reading the word in context, thereby understanding the intent of the user.

A personal definition is a definition that an individual selects from all of the descriptions and synonyms that the person believes could apply to a perception. This selection is heavily influenced by the individual's database, emotions, and personal point of view. A personal definition may be purely objective, it may follow an accepted, popular interpretation, or it may be a unique spin, made with or without concern for accuracy or political correctness.

Personal definitions can be engineered to support any perspective. If an individual perspective (a point of view pertaining to a specific subject) conflicts with your desired primary perspective (how you choose to interpret the world around you), it can be made more compatible through such engineering. This is accomplished by first examining the personal definitions that you have attached to that individual perspective, then doing your best to redefine those definitions that conflict with the bigger picture.

By successfully improving your personal definitions, an internal conflict can be resolved without changing the circumstances that initiated it. You merely rearrange your interpretations. Instead of waiting for the core creators of your stress to disappear. You engineer a perspective that no longer sees them as problems.

Many years ago, I attended a seminar put on by a well-known entrepreneur. He told the audience that when pursuing goals, we should remind ourselves, "I'm going to die someday." His intent was to emphasize the fact that life is short and that we shouldn't take it lightly.

He said that most peoples' concerns are trivial and that we should not let them limit our potential.

After hearing these words, I began to think about all the tedious, workaday things that were interfering with my personal ambitions, and I realized I had been ignoring the importance of my limited time. I used that speaker's fatalistic statement as my kick-in-the-butt to begin some earnest goal setting. However, as well as prompting me to plan new possibilities for my life, my new dedication also added new anxieties. I began to view time as grains of sand draining through the neck of an hourglass. As I sprinted toward the finish line, I became obsessed with life's finale rather than its melody, and this resulted in time seeming to pass by even more quickly.

The speaker's message wasn't wrong. How I had applied it was wrong. It was true, I would die someday, therefore my time deserved the highest respect, but I shouldn't have used that realization to make my life more complex.

Thankfully, I found a way to have it all, a way to continue my ambitions without experiencing their previously negative effect. The pursuit of my goals became enjoyable, rather than stressful, once I converted negative experiences into positive ones simply by altering a few of my personal definitions.

Here is an example to demonstrate how personal definitions combine to create an individual perspective, and how the greater, primary perspective is affected as a result:

Personal Definitions:

1) In order to be happy, I must achieve my goals.
2) A goal requires sacrifice.
3) Time is short.

Resulting Individual perspective: The goal process is stressful.

Effect on the Primary Perspective: A negative influence.

Do you see how personal definitions and perspectives are interrelated? Now let me show you how even small changes to each of the aforementioned personal definitions would significantly improve the resulting individual perspective and its effect on the primary perspective:

Altered Personal Definitions:

1) Achieving a goal will add to my happiness.
2) Working hard for a reward is stimulating.
3) Every moment is special.

Resulting Individual Perspective: The goal process is rewarding.

Effect on the Primary Perspective: A positive influence.

By making slight alterations to your stress-causing personal definitions, you can undo their negative effect on your primary perspective. The altered definitions used in the second example are completely compatible with the first example's definitions. Neither falsehoods nor deceits were used to bring about a change in perspective. Instead, minor, truthful revisions were used to dramatically improve the net effect. A slight variation to your personal definitions can make a huge difference in how you feel.

Just as definitions ultimately determine one's perspective, the reverse also occurs. A point of view such as "Life is special" automatically attracts positive definitions to support that interpretation. A perspective is self-perpetuating, whether it be positive or negative, because definitions and perspectives interrelate to nourish each other.

Your life experience will effectively improve if you create definitions that take away tension, rather than adding stress. Even aggravating stimuli can be defused by responding with the right personal definitions. With a little creativity, life can be experienced your way instead of it being a matter of happenstance.

It's important to keep in mind that in every case there are two ways to redefine a negative: 1) You can use redefining skills to directly attack the negative itself, altering its definition to make it less imposing; or 2)

You can leave the negative alone and work instead on redefining its effect on you. The first approach is aimed at erasing the negative, so that it then becomes a non-issue, while the second targets your response to the negative, helping you to cope with something that is perhaps too strong to define away. If one approach doesn't work, try the other. One of these two methods is certain to bring a positive result.

Consider this scenario: Let's say you are an introvert who fears social gatherings. You have just moved into a new community, and a neighbor invites you to a costume Halloween party. Prior to knowing how to make your life better by coming up with beneficial personal definitions, you would have immediately felt stressed, and believed you were in a no-win situation. But this time —ZAP!— the word "perspective" flashes into your mind, reminding you that you are in control of your interpretations. With your new insight, you are no longer limited to your old way of doing things. First you consider your options:

1) You can accept the invitation, so that you don't offend your neighbor, even though you'd rather not go.
2) You can turn down the invitation and stay at home.
3) You can replace your anxiety with positive definitions and then begin planning your costume.

Out of these three possibilities, which do you think is the best choice? You are probably guessing the third one, because you think, "That's what I should do." Actually, any of these three options has the potential to work either for you or against you. Each answer could be right or wrong. The best choice is the one that leaves you feeling the most comfortable. The most important factor for any personal decision is being at peace with it.

Insecurities and phobias can overpower a good intention. Forcing yourself to do something that leaves you feeling stressed isn't the best way to enjoy the moment. Even if you undergo a changeover, you will never completely alter who you are. If you are an introvert, each of the three previous options contains negative elements that are impossible to eliminate. A negative perception can always be improved, but completely getting rid of it… that's asking quite a lot. It might seem as if there's no perfect solution. However, before giving up and popping a Xanax, the new-and-improved you will first try using personal definitions to help resolve this conundrum. Here are examples of constructive personal definitions that could give each option a happy ending:

Regarding Option #1

Perception: *I am uncomfortable at social gatherings. Attending this party would be a huge negative. But, if I say 'No,' my new neighbor will be offended, and that would also be a huge negative.*

Constructive Personal Definitions: *"I am not ruled by fear. New experiences are stimulating. This isn't that big a deal. Accepting this invitation is the right thing to do, and it will create good feelings between me and my neighbor. I am a considerate person. I will have a good time."*

Decision: *My strength will overcome my weakness, and I will come out of this just fine. I will go to the party, and I will look for the positives in the moment. Meanwhile, I won't dwell on it; instead, I will RELAX.*

Regarding Option #2

Perception: *I have choices in my life, and I'm free to choose those that make me feel best. No creative definitions can overcome the negative feelings I have about social gatherings.*

Constructive Personal Definitions: *It's not possible to completely eliminate my negative perceptions of this party. It's better to prevent stress than to cope with it. It's important that I prioritize my own emotional well-being.*

Decision: *If I decide to go, I'll be stressed from now until the party is over. If I don't do well at the party, I'll feel embarrassed. I don't need that! The best option for me is to stay home and RELAX.*

Regarding Option #3

Perception: *My nature is to avoid this party, but through the power of personal definitions, I have the ability to change what would have been a negative situation into a positive experience.*

Constructive Personal Definitions: *This invitation is an opportunity, not a stress. Attending will help me lose my fear of social gatherings. The party will be interesting. After the event is over, I will feel more comfortable in my new community.*

Decision: *I will go to the party and have a nice time. It won't be stressful, because throughout the evening I'll make positive definitions that will allow me to RELAX.*

You don't have to be the clone of a promoted psychological or sociological ideal in order to have a healthy mindset. In the shaping of your own mental health, you have flexibility. Your specific choices are not that critical as long as your selections support the feelings you are after, thereby contributing to a healthy, happy state of mind. Isn't that your ultimate goal? Therefore, you don't have to follow what someone else says you should do. You just need to decide what it is that you want to feel, what will bring that feeling, and then go after it. It's entirely up to you.

Negatives and prejudices can exist within an Ultimate Perspective. An Ultimate Perspective doesn't have to live up to any ideal or to any moral code. A thought that is perceived to be a negative by someone else could be just what you need in your life to bring order out of chaos. The concept for you to grasp is the importance of attaining an outlook—whatever it takes—that helps you feel mentally healthy as often as possible.

We have the ability to define for ourselves what things fall into the categories of "positives" and "negatives." This results in individuality, adaptability, and unlimited versatility. Each person's experiences and beliefs are unique, therefore it's not possible to mass produce any singular point of view. Governments and religions that have attempted to do so have repeatedly failed. Any healthy individual can be happy, regardless of his abilities, when he nurtures his own needs, rather than trying to conform to the visions of others. "You see, you can't please everyone, so you got to please yourself." -Ricky Nelson.

REALIZATION: Ultimate Perspectives do not follow a blueprint.

***

Any improvement to your happiness is a victory. Whenever the balance begins to tip toward the positive, you feel stronger, and if you add positives while at the same time lightening the weight of negatives, even better things begin to happen. The achievement of an Ultimate Perspective will not eliminate every negative that haunts you, but positives will rule.

The Cadillac of Ultimate Perspectives would be "Everything is wonderful all the time." If that's your general outlook, then it'll take quite a lot to ruin your day. An Ultimate Perspective doesn't have to be that idealistic. It just has to be good enough to keep the negatives at bay, and to produce positive feelings the majority of the time.

REALIZATION: Ultimate Perspectives are weighted with positives, but that doesn't mean they are perfections.

***

Needs and interests change over time, and as they do, an Ultimate Perspective will gradually remodel, adapting to the new definitions that are brought in. There is a negative to this adaptability, however: If one is not careful how new input is defined, an Ultimate Perspective can reshape into a self-defeating perspective once again.

You can tell if this is happening by how you feel. If you find peace waning, it's because you have drifted off course and allowed negative definitions to influence your thoughts. Thankfully, negative thoughts are your own creation, therefore you can pull out of these times by making course corrections (redefinitions) that improve your perspective and return you to an optimum state once again.

REALIZATION: Ultimate Perspectives are malleable.

***

You will learn that it's easy to find facts to support improved definitions. Sometimes all it takes is setting aside your prejudices, so you can look more objectively at the facts. In most instances, the facts are not the cause of your negative definitions; your biases are the culprits. They distort what would otherwise be innocent information, and transform it into something that's troublesome for you.

Obviously, existing positive perceptions don't require redefining, as do the negatives, but their benefit will be enhanced if you can raise the status of each one. Whenever you become aware of a fact that reinforces your goal, it's good to mentally highlight that perception before moving on to your next consideration. Recognize it as a benefit to your outlook. Becoming aware of a positive, and then taking a moment to give it your appreciation, helps that positive to be imprinted in your mind, and, therefore, to increase its power of influence. Positive recognition helps solidify positive feelings.

Whenever your attention is drawn to something that you perceive to be a negative, you can change how it is affecting you by redefining it in a way that either: 1) converts it into a positive; 2) eliminates its importance; or 3) tempers its influence.

Making improved definitions for facts that you initially interpret as "negatives" requires somewhat of an artistic touch, but you can become a Picasso. What you must learn is how to place a positive spin on facts that are antagonistic toward your desired perspective, so they then become compatible with it.

Novelists and stand-up comedians are some of the very best storytellers. They have a knack for taking the commonplace and describing it in a way that's entertaining. These artists are able to elicit positive responses through creative renditions of reality.

For example, an average person might read a diary and find nothing in it but a mundane recollection of events, while a biographer could take the same account, put it into a colorful narrative, and earn the Nobel Prize for Literature. A store manager might watch a supermarket's security monitor and see nothing but monotonous grocery shopping all day long, while a stand-up comedian could watch the same monitor and find all kinds of hilarious material to use in his next monologue.

Your interpretation of the world around you is different from everyone else's. Without realizing it, you place your own spin on everything you take in. That spin is vitally important to how you end up feeling. Since you have the option to pick and choose your interpretations, why not select a rendition of the facts that puts things in the best possible light? The story you write for yourself can also be worthy of a Nobel Prize. It is your choice whether that tale is a documentary, drama, romantic comedy, action/adventure, or any other theme. You are limited only by your desire and your creativity.

It can be tough to know where to begin one's story. Old emotions and rusty images resist change, and it's difficult to identify deep-seated definitions that need alteration when those interpretations have sat comfortably in your head for many years. For some, a rebuilding is easy, but for others, perspective imperfections weigh too heavily. For those struggling against a barrage of negatives, it can be difficult to have faith that any improvement can be made.

If you attempt to see things more positively, but find you cannot break free from a negative state of mind, it may be because your environment has you in a negative grip. If so, it might be necessary to physically escape those imprisoning influences. If you have difficulty initiating a positive change, seek out an "alpine meadow," a place that has positive vibrations which will set the stage for positive creative thinking. Take an hour-long walk. Sit on the bank of a river. Do whatever you must do to initiate the task with a positive mindset. Even a few minutes spent in a more positive setting can make all the difference.

Your first steps may be somewhat of a Catch-22, because discovering a positive attitude requires having a little of it to begin with.

Trying to envision better possibilities while lying in bed or sitting at your desk might be a far-too-familiar setting that ties you to old, negative feelings. Set yourself up for a positive start by doing something you enjoy or by going someplace associated with pleasant memories. Find a way to create as good a moment as possible, and then make a promise to yourself that things are going to get better. Believe that you can make it happen. Generate a positive spark that will jumpstart an improved attitude, and then don't look back.

You are learning that through the power of reasoning, a perspective can be permanently altered. It is one of the few aspects of the psyche that's open to immediate restructuring; it only requires a simple editing of old information and the addition of new realizations. By intentionally fine-tuning your perspective, you can significantly change how things affect you.

You need new ideas that bring new feelings, therefore avoid old distractions. Your endeavor is a very personal one, so don't allow others to interfere. In particular, don't let someone else determine what you should believe. Your perspective decisions are solely yours to make, so be smart and don't let the ramblings of so-called "experts" keep you from doing what you know in your heart is right. Don't allow those with a diminished capacity for living or those with more superficial goals to pull you back into self-defeating beliefs and prejudices. Your objective is to succeed where they have failed. Remain firm in this quest. This aspiration will distinguish you from the rest of the crowd. You will be the one to set the mark. You will become the one with the wisdom to guide others toward a better life.

Beginning with as uncluttered a vision as is possible, be discriminating when building your foundation of new definitions. Think twice before applying labels impulsively. Instead of accepting your immediate impressions as truths, try qualifying your thoughts by asking yourself questions such as:

What would I think if I had no allegiance?

(examining the information from a broader perspective)

or

How would it affect me if my race were different?

(determining if the information is prejudiced)

You are the only one who can determine what information is or isn't compatible with your primary perspective goal. If something seems to be an ill fit, redefine it before endorsing it or allowing it to be catalogued in your mind as "fact." Strive to make good definitions as you go, for every time your mind skips to the next thought, it automatically stores the image and feelings that have just been experienced. Make it right the first time, so you won't have to rework it later. If you can't determine how something should be interpreted, place your definition on hold for future resolution. You are better off to delay placing labels, rather than to assign improper ones that could recycle your analytical base back to its beginning.

You are probably thinking: *Analyzing a lifetime's accumulation of personal definitions, and then coming up with creative, new definitions for the thousands that have a negative impact... that would be impossible!* You are absolutely right. Your brain would explode long before you could complete such a task. Only the most prominent roadblocks should be met head on at first. Lesser self-defeating definitions can be undone "on the fly" as they happen to pop up, and as your conscious mind becomes increasingly positive, your subconscious mind will automatically take care of many others that have subtly wrought damage over the years.

You also might be wondering: *How do I know what definitions are best for me?* The answer lies deep within you. Your Ultimate Perspective is not about objectivity, it's about feelings. Your inner soul knows what it needs. Give it some credit. Give it some time. Your logical, computing brain may be less reliable than your gut feelings in determining those essentials, for your mind has been too heavily influenced, and it has too many options to consider. Listen to the whisperings of your heart and your conscience. If a definition feels right, go with it and believe in it. You don't have to think mechanically. Allow yourself to feel as you make your definitions.

Your next question is likely: *How can I have faith in my inner voice when I've made such a mess of things so far?* With time comes experience, and with both come maturity and wisdom. As a child, you had neither the maturity nor the wisdom to accurately interpret every new experience, and almost everything that happened was new to you in one regard or another. Misinterpretations and immature emotions have been responsible for most of the faulty data on your hard drive. Now that you have wizened, your childhood impressions can be reworked. Your past reasoning isn't indicative of your current abilities. You will do much better this time around.

Insight improves when you look at the big picture. When you were a child, that picture was not all that big. The more time that went by, the greater the contents of that picture. When young, you thought moment-by-moment; you didn't have years of experience to rely on for help, so you made many errors in judgment. As you became older, you learned from your trials, and acquired understandings that only experience could provide.

It would seem that the more experiences we have, the more acute our observations would be. However, that's not always the case, since many early-life events are poorly interpreted when they happen, thereby distorting future reasoning. A young mind is open, but immature. An adult mind is mature, but rife with biases. There is no ideal age for interpreting the world. For you, the best age is your age, and the best time is now.

It takes discipline and self-control to stay positive when negatives are continually attempting to undermine your attitude. That's why it's so important to make a habit of maintaining your perspective each day.

A contented state of mind can easily be taken for granted. You must have perspective awareness during the good times so that you are ready to go should things begin to fall apart.

If your thoughts stay tuned to the concept of a positive primary perspective, then you will remain programmed to constructively deal with whatever comes your way. All you will have to do when frustration or depression surfaces is to remind yourself that you have the ability to do something about it, then use your redefining skills to bring back your rainbow.

A time of duress is a magnificent opportunity for discovering the treasure trove of everyday positives that are essential for lasting happiness. Simple positives become more apparent during and after a period of pain, fear, or heartache, because those common essentials are more recognizable when you are hungering for any good moment. When you are at a low point, you have longings that reach out, eager to grab whatever will bring relief. When the world seems more dark than light, the most accessible positives are the small items that are overlooked when happy perceptions are rolling your way. Because everyday positives are the most abundant and most easily accessible positives, those are the ones most likely to initiate a rescue during a time of crisis.

Ultimate Perspective Key #3:

THE KEY TO A DURABLE HAPPINESS IS SEEING THE BEAUTY IN EVERYDAY THINGS.

A crisis isn't the only time when everyday positives can come to your rescue. The common stresses that keep you on edge can be surmounted, or at least made translucent, by doing nothing more than heightening your appreciation for the positives you already have. If you become accustomed to appreciating the simple things, contentment will be the norm. Remember, you cannot feel both good and bad at the same time.

Whenever you are down, ask yourself: *Why am I feeling this way? What will it take to make me feel better? Is there a better way to interpret what's happening to me?* Try to come up with a more positive spin, even if you think it will do little good. Begin with the negatives that are making the most noise, the things that make you feel the worst. Could there be some good hidden within the storm? Might there be a rainbow to anticipate? Rewrite the negative aspects of your problem. Write in some positives. Don't allow things that are irrelevant to squeeze your brain! By improving your perspective, any situation will improve. Augmenting your primary perspective will not guarantee that roses will be sent your way, but it will certainly help you grow your own.

When constructing your Ultimate Perspective, remind yourself that there's nothing that should not be given a second look. You have hundreds of beliefs that could be redefined for the better. Your goal is to build a primary perspective that will result in good feelings. You must forever put aside those things that are incompatible with a positive outlook or that are impossible to redefine. You have no space in your mind for such trash! Hopeless, negative thoughts are not worth a second of your time.

Put your energy towards self-determination. Let it be the focus of your life. Begin to make improvements everywhere possible. Even items that you think are "the good things" should be reconsidered. You need to make sure that what you assume to be positives are not negatives in disguise, and if they are true positives, try making them even better.

I don't know about you, but I'm greedy. I'm not content with "OK," I want "Great!" America has always been a breeding ground for overachievers, and I was raised in that mold. I see no problem in finding happiness amid an atmosphere of high expectations and a striving for exceptional results. Why should anyone settle for a comfortable perspective when it's possible to experience an extraordinary one? A perspective should be a rewarding outlook without empty spaces, one that enhances "the good life."

Your moments are shaped by your definitions, therefore you control how great those moments become. But even if you achieve an exceptionally positive outlook, that doesn't mean you can let down your guard. Negatives are tenacious. They can be downgraded, but they will incessantly attempt to regain their power over you. Also, there will always be contrary perspectives in competition with yours, guaranteeing perpetual conflict, and some that are similar to yours today will be dissimilar tomorrow as you reformat into a new person. The outside world is not going to change with you. Negatives will continually attempt to undo your accomplishments. They are opportunistic, and most likely to attack when your back is turned.

Consider this analogy: A gardener begins with a plot of compacted earth and weeds. He clears the area, turns the soil, and buries the seeds that will become vegetables for harvest. He then cultivates the soil throughout the growing season to control the opportunistic weeds that would otherwise compete with his growing plants. The more frequent his weeding, the easier the task and, ultimately, the more bountiful his crop. He knows that even when his vegetables appear to be thriving, weeds cannot be ignored, because if left unchecked, they can quickly overwhelm even a healthy garden, and return the ground to its original, wild state.

The garden of your mind will constantly be invaded by negatives that will need weeding so that good feelings will grow. The cultivation you do will determine the health of your garden. In order to maintain your perspective, you must recognize those things that conflict with your vision, and then define them in a way that blocks them from stealing the nutrients you need for a positive mindset.

Present-day negatives are not the only threat. Old negatives will occasionally rise from their graves to haunt you. You'll never fully suppress your accustomed, negative definitions. To believe that you can would be an illusion. Just as a former smoker or alcoholic must continually resist being pulled back into old, destructive habits, so must you resist the unraveling of your positive achievements.

After you attain a positive perspective, don't become complacent and allow it to fade. Never stop looking for positives. Be determined to continually substantiate a positive outlook. This life is your one chance; there will not be a second opportunity. Remember, positives breed positives, and negatives breed negatives. Work at reducing negative thoughts.

RETENTION: Commit to a lifelong effort.

*****

Remain aware that your success sets you apart from the masses. You can't allow the shortcomings and frustrations of others to interfere with doing what's necessary to foster your own well-being. Selfishness, in this instance, is morally acceptable, for you can only be a positive influence on others after you have first achieved your own positive mindset.

RETENTION: Resist the collective mindset.

*****

It takes no effort to trip and fall, but getting back on your feet can be a strain, especially if you've injured yourself. A perspective setback can temporarily knock you off your feet. It can strike like a lightning bolt, quickly and unexpectedly. Count on it happening! When a perspective setback occurs, it may stun you at first, but you have the ability to regain your balance. Do not be disillusioned. Just keep in mind the following:

1) Life is priceless.
2) Time is a limited resource, so it must be used wisely.
3) This moment is your most important moment.
4) You must continually seek out positives.
5) Your past beliefs are not set in stone.
6) You are in control of your perceptions and definitions.
7) Being happy is your top priority.

RETENTION: Prepare to be challenged.

In order to accelerate your perspective changeover, here's what I suggest: First, take out a paper and pen once again, and list a few words or short phrases that express how you would like to feel the majority of the time. Next, list a few of your present personal definitions, both positives and negatives (simple ones, not major players).

Your first list describes your perspective goal. Save this for future reference. The second list contains definitions to begin evaluating. Ask yourself: *Are these definitions compatible with the words that describe how I'd like to feel?* You will probably see that some will support your goal, while others will work against it. Obviously, the compatible ones will not have to be redefined, but see what you can do to improve those that are antagonistic to your goal. Here are some examples:

YOU WOULD LIKE TO FEEL: Relaxed, Happy, Energetic.

Random personal definition: *Loud people are annoying.*
Solution/Redefinition: Soften your definition to lessen the relevance of this annoyance, i.e. *Loud people are minor nuisances that are irrelevant to my state of mind.*

YOU WOULD LIKE TO FEEL: Relaxed, Happy, Energetic.

Random personal definition: *Rainy days are depressing.*

Solution/redefinition: Choose a definition that is more positive, i.e. *Rainy days are peaceful and relaxing.*

YOU WOULD LIKE TO FEEL: Relaxed, Happy, Energetic.

Random personal definition: *Winter is a fun time of year.*

Solution/redefinition: No changes needed. Go dust off the sled!

There's no topic that cannot be perceived from several different angles. Before forming an opinion, consider the possibilities and select definitions that improve how you either interpret or accept each situation. Remember, a personal definition does not have to be factually based, you simply must believe in it. However, I encourage you to rely on truth when it's apparent. An argument could be made that truth isn't important, as long as one's point of view is benefited, but you will ultimately pay a hefty price if you deceive yourself, since the perspectives that arise from deceit inevitably fail when challenged. The only way that you can be sure that your definitions will never let you down is to find facts that substantiate them.

***

Applying *The Changeover's* "Three Rs:"

REGOGNITION: At this point you recognize what you must do. As you continue throughout the next days, months, and years, you will grow an understanding of the stimuli that influence your emotions, so that through your personal defining skills, you will be able to adapt them to meet your emotional goals.

REALIZATION: Once a positive primary perspective has been realized, you will enjoy a new attitude, where situations that once troubled you are no longer as troublesome, and where peace and happiness are your realities.

RETENTION: After establishing your Ultimate Perspective, you will retain your improved attitude and not slip back into a self-defeating perspective. You will consistently enjoy each moment by maintaining your improved insight.

***

Revisiting the keys to an Ultimate Perspective:

THE KEY TO MENTAL WELL-BEING IS ATTAINING A POSITIVE PRIMARY PERSPECTIVE.

Perspective is everything! How you see yourself and the world around you determines your attitude and the emotions that result. A negative perspective poisons your thinking ability, and interferes with the accumulation of the positive interpretations that are essential for life fulfillment. To enjoy maximum mental health, you must attain a positive primary perspective.

THE KEY TO A POSITIVE PERSPECTIVE IS CREATING POSITIVE PERSONAL DEFINTIONS.

You are burdened with the input that your brain has received throughout your lifetime, and once impressions have been formed, they don't change on their own. However, you have the ability to intentionally alter how you interpret those impressions, and thereby change how they affect you. A positive perspective requires positive interpretations. The only way to see the world in a better light is to increase the percentage of positive personal definitions stored in your brain.

THE KEY TO A DURABLE HAPPINESS IS SEEING THE BEAUTY IN EVERYDAY THINGS.

During a "special" moment, happiness is a no-brainer. Out-of-the-ordinary times like birthdays, holidays, and vacations are easily perceived as being positive, but those moments quickly come and go. Happiness should last and not be the exception. A durable happiness can only be realized by learning to appreciate the simple things, the routine living that you experience each and every day.

9

Appreciation

Appreciate:

To *Value* justly; to be *Aware* of; to be *Grateful* for.

Regarding *Value*: Something's value depends on how it compares to other items. An everyday event is typically perceived as having a relatively low value when compared to an event that comes along only occasionally. An item that is expensive, and thereby requires more sacrifice to be afforded, is valued more than an item that is easily attainable. So, it would seem there's a problem: How can the value of common, everyday experiences ever approach that of the less frequent, "special" experiences? Must we falsify our definitions and deceive ourselves into believing that everyday moments are more significant than they really are? How can we honestly appreciate something that we customarily take for granted?

Regarding *Awareness*: We notice sand burrs when our bare feet step on them. Salt is noticed when a food contains either too much or too little. Many things go unnoticed until they grab our attention in some obvious way. More recognition is given to hurricanes than to soft breezes. We are fascinated by a fireworks display, but we pay little attention to the stars shining in the background. There's so much to perceive in life that a mind has to prioritize its attention. Since it's not possible to absorb everything, how do we become more aware of the common positives?

Regarding *Grateful*: We are grateful for what we appreciate. We appreciate what we value or covet. Things that are common-place are usually overlooked when counting our blessings. How can we be grateful for things that we customarily take for granted?

Since you have the ability to take charge of your thoughts, perhaps you can become more appreciative simply by making it your resolution. You could try repeating the mantra, "I will appreciate the everyday things." Would that work for you? If you think it might, let's test this hypothesis by adding some realism. Let's see if you would be willing to commit yourself to "I will appreciate mundane living." How long do you think you could live up to such a resolution? A vow is difficult to uphold when it requires that you act contrary to your accustomed mindset.

It's just not possible to be appreciative by intent alone. There must be substance to support such a state of mind. You must truly believe that life is a positive experience in order for a positive mental attitude to be genuine. Only when you are authentically grateful do appreciations come naturally, therefore to recognize everyday beauty, you must acquire an honest appreciation for everyday things.

Perceived value will vary depending on one's needs. Visualize an old, weathered prospector wandering aimlessly across a barren desert. The sun is beating down relentlessly. The temperature is 112 degrees, and he has been without water since he sucked the last drop out of his canteen two days ago. His lips are cracked and crusty, and his tongue is like sandpaper against his palate. As the exhausted man labors over the top of a rise, he unexpectedly comes upon this sign:

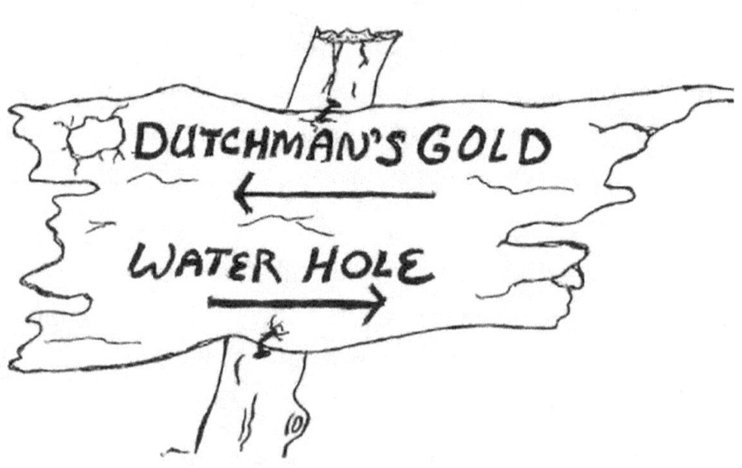

At that moment, it's very clear which direction he should go, but the choice isn't ours to make. It's up to him to determine what's most valuable. His crisis has narrowed his focus, but his ambitions could still blind him. He's probably confused, especially if he has been conditioned to value gold more than anything else. But he sure is thirsty! As he stares at the sign, trying to figure which direction to take, the sun gets hotter and his knees get weaker. It's most likely that his need for water will overpower his avarice, and he'll choose the trail leading to life. The perceived value of water can be much higher than that of gold.

What determines something's true value? Regarding the simple things in life, we are pretty much dealing with *perceived* value, which is entirely a personal matter. What would you be willing to pay at a garage sale for a worn-out blanket? For use as a trunk liner, a dollar might be generous. But, what price would you be willing to pay for an old, frayed blanket if you were in a stalled car, stuck overnight during a snow storm?

Those things that are abundant and readily available are typically underappreciated. We perceive the items that are rare and difficult to obtain as always having the greatest value. This is a grave misconception. The potential value of an old blanket or a canteen full of water demonstrates that the common everyday things can be the most important of all.

Are you sensing what this means? Are you beginning to see the amazing opportunity that awaits you? Once you can perceive your common experiences as being special, imagine how you can indulge yourself, living only within the parameters that exist! You don't have to become rich. In fact, nothing has to change at all. All you have to do is become more appreciative of the abundance that already surround you.

During infancy, everything that happened to you was special. Being handed your first toy was the height of excitement. Eventually, your enthusiasm over the toy lessened somewhat, but it still held a relatively high value as long as it was your only plaything. Its perceived importance didn't significantly lessen until you began to accumulate other toys. As new items were added to your toy chest, that first toy became less and less valued and eventually forgotten. The toy didn't change; your valuation of the toy changed.

Most of what happens in life is similar, day in and day out. Our impressions of those repetitive experiences are what remodel over time. We who are fortunate enough to live with our basic needs satisfied are quick to lose interest and to change our priorities. We have a restless nature because we have been conditioned to achieve, rather than to be content. Because we want more than we currently have, routine living is undervalued and day-to-day appreciation is an improbability. We are good at searching for happiness, because we are good at taking action, but we cannot *be* happy. That requires acceptance, which is contrary to our nature.

Your environment needn't improve in order for you to find things to appreciate, nor do you have to imagine things to be better than they are. What you do have to do is recall the impact once made by those "toys" that you have depreciated. You don't need to acquire appreciation; you need to regain appreciation.

There was a time when you appreciated each and every item that you now find uninteresting, a time when you fully appreciated each experience. With the passing of time, your possessions and your moments have become devalued. However, this fact is not entirely a negative. As a result of these devaluations, countless appreciations are now available to you at bargain prices. They are everywhere and they are easily accessible.

You have to see things positively before you can be appreciative. Wait a minute…is this a chicken-or-the-egg quandary? Which is it: becoming positive in order to be appreciative, or being appreciative in order to become positive? How can one state of being exist without the other preceding it? Which is needed first?

It's true that once everything is spinning along, perception, appreciation, positive effect, and perspective interrelate to become a singular force. But although these things intertwine, perspective is the dominant factor because it is the final interpreter.

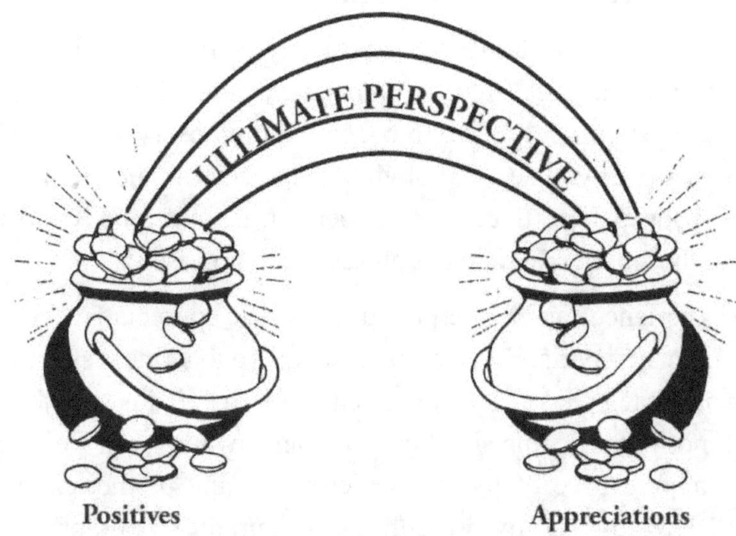

The majority of simple positives that are currently invisible to you will not come to light until you have achieved a more positive, Ultimate Perspective. Once you begin to experience a perspective that helps you notice more of the good around you, you will then have the ability to be more appreciative.

For appreciation to become part of your nature, each day a few moments should be allotted for reflection on the positives in your life, and when you count those blessings, do more than just scan through the obvious ones (God, love, friendships, etc.). Dig a little deeper as well to find some less-obvious blessings that will make your appreciation more complete. Just as "special" moments are too infrequent to keep you stimulated three hundred and sixty-five days a year, a few items of exceptional value will not provide you with a consistent sense of appreciation. Your goal is to develop a wide variety of appreciations.

An Ultimate Perspective is not fragile. Its survival isn't dependent on the continual addition of appreciations. However, the intensity of good feelings that a positive perspective provides increases further with each added appreciation. Once appreciations begin to grow, especially for the every-day things, you will feel more content, which, in turn, will lead to being even more appreciative. This is another cycle that continuously feeds a sense of well-being.

When you look for things to appreciate, you find them. If you allow yourself to relax and get into the moment, you can be grateful for the simplest things; you only have to become more observant and look for value in whatever you see. An obvious appreciation is certainly a nice plus for your perspective, but its benefit is multiplied when you recognize the smaller, associated pluses that comprise it.

An experience can be interpreted as a single appreciated event or as many appreciated parts. For example, when I go to a fine restaurant I try to appreciate each phase of the experience, for my goal is to enjoy every moment, not just the time spent chewing and swallowing. Beforehand, I can be appreciative of the clothes I put on and of the anticipatory feelings I have during my drive to the restaurant. Upon arrival, I can appreciate the restaurant décor, the table setting, the menu, the wait staff, and watching the other patrons. Later there's the afterglow, arriving back home, slipping into comfy clothes, and, lastly, slipping into comfy dreams. An appreciated event can add a single plus to your perspective or its benefit can be multiplied by raising the value of all those little things that comprise it. It's up to you whether an appreciation is a spark or a flame.

The real world isn't the only resource for limitless things to appreciate. Memories also contain a treasure trove of positives, and those memories can be appreciated over and over again. In fact, appreciating a past moment can be as good for your attitude as appreciating something in the present.

Recently, I had some time to kill while sitting in a waiting room. I had nothing pressing to think about, so I searched my mental archives for an enjoyable rerun. The memory that happened to pop up was of the first date I had with my wife many years ago. Instead of casually reviewing the event, I decided to make a game of it and see how much detail I could recall of the whole experience. In replaying it, I became aware that each phase of the evening had something to appreciate.

When the rerun was over, after I had recalled as many exceptional and simple moments as I could, I decided to once more revisit a few of those images to determine which was most special to me. In doing so, I realized that the moment that stood out above all others that night was a brief, silent time when I sat mesmerized at the dinner table, entrapped by the beauty of my wife's lovely eyes. That memory revived my original feelings. The appreciation of a simple positive in the past can add greatly to your general sense of appreciation in the present.

There are so many blessings to be counted, so many reasons to sincerely enjoy the moment. Love, friendship, comfort, pleasure, and beauty are all readily accessible to you. Goodness can be found in things as simple as pausing to rest, tasting food, feeling warmth, feeling coolness, hearing rain tapping on a rooftop, or basking in the sun's healing rays. There are always fond memories to recall, and there are always dreams that might come true.

Substituting appreciations for negativity prevents you from being consumed by unpleasant thoughts, and there are countless positives awaiting your appreciation. Remember this whenever you feel negativity gnawing at your soul. Remain cognizant of the fact that there is no end to what you can appreciate, so that your positive mental attitude will be enduring.

Whenever you weaken and your thoughts turn negative, you must break away from that mindset. Put on the brakes, so that you go no further, then defend your well-being by telling yourself: *Look at all there is to appreciate. I'm fine. There are many reasons to feel good. I won't allow negatives to destroy me or my precious moments.*

Regardless of the positives available, many of us have the perception that we haven't made the grade, and that others are much better off. If you hold these thoughts, you have work to do. First, tell your ego "Get lost," then take a more objective look at yourself. See if you can find facts that will support a better self-perception. On this Earth there are tens of thousands, if not millions, who would trade places with you in an instant if they could, especially now that you are developing a better life perspective, something those whom you have been envying may never attain. You could be much worse off. You are not someone else's property. You are not in an entirely hopeless situation. You either have—or you have the potential to have—family, friends, health, safety, and all of life's possibilities. Why underrate that potential when it's only beginning to emerge? No amount of wealth or fame can match the fulfillment that awaits you, providing you are willing to open your arms to a perspective that is appreciative.

Recap To This Point:

1) Your life is a continuum of moments more precious than the rarest gems or the most cherished works of art. Enjoying the moment is everything.

2) Humanity is experiencing rapid cultural change. You live in a stressful era when contentment is becoming increasingly elusive.

3) There are good reasons for differing perspectives. You can better understand yourself and others by taking a closer look at why you think and act the way you do.

4) Your ego is responsible for many definitions that are not necessarily founded on truth. Those interpretations prevent you from being open-minded and from accurately defining your world.

5) Your definitions determine your perspective. You have the ability to redefine those things that do not fit your desired vision. Your perspective is vitally important and should be thoughtfully examined.

6) The development of an appreciative nature fosters the ability to recognize the beauty surrounding you. By realizing that simple things are valuable and worthy of your appreciation, you will incur an honest, more positive view of life.

10

Humility

As stated in Chapter 1, the purpose of *The Changeover* is not to improve how other people perceive you. The objective is to improve your own vision, specifically how you view yourself. But the image you project to others does have relevancy, for what you show them is a representation of what you are feeling. When you are ill, you project fragility; when you are frustrated, you project exasperation; when you are content, you project humility.

Most of us are raised to be proud. It's our heritage. Our culture encourages significance and recognition. In an achievement-oriented society, accomplishment is the measure of an individual's worth. It's contrary to our conditioning to downplay talent and achievement, something that would require choosing humility over pride. Most of us would rather be seen as being pretentious than as insignificant. Although a degree of bravado can be acceptable, it's preferable that an ego be relatively unobtrusive, what's referred to as a "healthy ego."

Every ego needs praise because that's what egos are all about. For your ego to be satisfied, it needs a full tank of high-octane approval. The source of that approval isn't important as long as the tank can stay filled. Through self-appreciation you have the ability to manufacture 100% of your own fuel, but if you don't produce enough, your ego will look elsewhere for satiation. Friends and loved ones are good resources for additional fuel because they are the ones most likely to be benevolent, but that benevolence is proportional to their own sense of well-being. Outsiders are an option, but even more so than with friends and loved ones, outsiders are an uncertain resource because most have their own ego insufficiencies to satisfy.

A contented ego is fuel-efficient, has a small tank to fill, requires little maintenance, and produces few noxious emissions. People with contented egos don't seek praise. They don't need affirmation of their worth. But as long as there's an ego of any kind, healthy or unhealthy, there remains a constant need for fuel.

Earlier, I spent time emphasizing your relative insignificance in the scheme of things. I did this to increase your humility. Those who are humble experience less stress and are more content than those who require praise. The greater your humility, the happier you are in every regard. Humility provides a calming effect. It allows you a wider perspective, so that you are better able to see beyond yourself. If you believe that you are something greater than you are, or that you are deserving of special treatment, then you are setting yourself up for discontent. When people believe they are "due," as in "I deserve more," that perception guarantees inner conflict. It provokes a fruitless war of avarice vs. magnanimity that perpetuates frustration. When you feel humility, there's no need for pretension. By accepting yourself as you are, you don't have to worry about measuring up or feeling inadequate when you fail to perform beyond your abilities.

***

Beauties on Bourbon Street

Kimberly Lovely, Miss Gulf Coast, has been anticipating the upcoming national beauty pageant for a long time—in fact, as long as she can remember. For the past twelve months she has been counting and recounting calories, and she has been exercising daily with her sadistic trainer, Barney Bell. Kim has done everything possible to enhance her already stunning beauty, including giving Dr. Smiley a considerable sum to change all of her silver fillings to porcelain.

The preliminaries start tomorrow at noon, so Kim will be meeting with her hair stylist and the rest of the cosmetic team at 8 AM to begin putting the finishing touches on her transformation. But for now, all that can be done has been done, so this evening she will try her best to just rest and stay calm.

Kim has been through a lot this year. Self-sacrifice has been the norm. You can probably imagine the stress she has already put herself through, but can you imagine the turmoil she will be experiencing tomorrow night? Her lifelong dream will be on the line. She has invested so much time and energy, all to compete in an event where the odds are fifty to one against her, where there can only be one winner and the rest "also-rans." What do you suppose those last few moments will be like for Kim, waiting for the judges to announce their decision?

In contrast to Kimberly's moments, imagine those of Cookie Humble. She has come to New Orleans with her husband, Guido, for a well-deserved getaway: a fun-filled weekend that includes a tour of the French Quarter, Dixieland on Bourbon Street, luxurious hotel facilities, and attendance at the beauty pageant.

Cookie could easily have been a beauty queen, herself. All her life her exceptional loveliness has caused jaws to drop. In her senior year of high school, she was voted "Homecoming Queen" and "Best Personality." Twenty years later, she can still hardly cross the street without stopping traffic. Yet, despite all that attention, Cookie has never tried to market her popularity or her good looks. In fact, she is embarrassed whenever she gets attention. She has always been appreciative of the compliments that come her way, but her choices in life have never been influenced by a desire for recognition.

Tomorrow night at the pageant, Cookie and Guido will be sitting together, happily taking in all the glitz and glamour. Cookie is anxious to see the fabulous gowns that the women will be wearing. She certainly is not worried about keeping Guido happy, because she knows he will enjoy looking at…well, we know it won't be the designer shoes! No matter how the evening unfolds, it's safe to presume that Cookie's experience will be vastly more relaxing than that of Kimberly.

Kimberly and Cookie may appear equally gracious, but Cookie is the one with the greater inner humility. Cookie's ego is the type that requires less fuel and, as a result, her evening at the pageant will contain much less stress. Her happiness will not depend on who ends up winning. There's a huge contrast in emotions experienced between those who elect to be on stage and those who prefer to be in the audience.

There's a huge contrast between having a needy ego and having inner humility.

Easter Funday

Last spring an aspiring, yet-to-be-recognized gourmet chef named Peter Panache went to work at 4 AM to prepare Easter brunch. He had worked well into the evening the night before, taking care of all the last-minute details so that the holiday feast would go off without a hitch. This was sure to be a long day. Although technically not much different from last week's Sunday brunch (and the one scheduled for next week, and those planned for every Sunday thereafter), this highly visible day was an opportunity to showcase his superstar potential. Developing a good reputation is everything to someone who does not yet have one, and so the pressure was on.

Five minutes before the 11 AM opening, the cooks were hurrying to put the finishing touches on the wonderful dishes that were being shuttled to the buffet for the throngs of patrons lined up at the front entrance. With one minute to go, the large floral bouquet on the pastry table was repositioned "just so," and with everything completed as planned, Peter dragged himself to the back of the kitchen and collapsed into a flour-dusted metal chair for a well-deserved break. Peter sure was exhausted, but he was also proud of his accomplishment, a deserved feeling to have. Late that afternoon, after the last brunch patrons had left with smiles on their faces, and after the kitchen and dining room had been thoroughly cleaned, Peter went home and promptly crawled into bed, not to awaken for the next twelve hours.

Peter wasn't the only person hoping that the Easter brunch would be a culinary marvel. Guido and Cookie were first in line that Easter morning. They were feeling great, aided by a good night's sleep and expectations for a stimulating day. After a light breakfast and an inspiring church service, they were eager to enjoy the long-anticipated brunch at their favorite restaurant.

At 11 AM sharp the doors opened, and they were graciously received by an attractive hostess who escorted them past the bounty of mouth-watering dishes to a window table overlooking the marina. Guido and Cookie then spent the next two hours dining on exceptional food, visiting tableside with friends, and watching the manatees that were feeding on water hyacinths by the quay outside their window. At the end of the meal, Guido looked at Cookie, gently took her hand, and said, "Sweetie, I love you so-o-o-o much! Happy Easter."

On this particular day, Peter was the benefactor of a job well done, and Guido and Cookie were the benefactors of Peter's hard work. Each was rewarded in some way by these contrasting experiences. It's not possible to say whose moments brought the most gratification, but, clearly, the more relaxing Easter Sunday belonged to Guido and Cookie, while most of the stress belonged to Peter.

***

We begin our adult lives performing services that we hope will provide us with the resources to be served ourselves one day. This progression doles out a lot of stress, but it's a stress that can be surmounted. Often times it's a matter of choice. There are those who choose to be in the race and those who choose to observe it. Some of us become the entertainers, others the audience. For the most part, people blessed with inner humility are those who prefer to be entertained. They're the ones who benefit from those whose lives are more chaotic.

Beauty pageants and other emotionally-charged, special events are not the only situations that compel people to create their own stress. One can enter a "how-do-I-measure-up?" contest every day, even several times each day. Decades of such self-imposed angst can make the eventual cessation of these concerns a much-needed relief. However, you need not reach retirement age to retire a significant portion of your stress. It can begin at any time by raising your personal humility. It's possible to discard many of the pressures that you've been under and become a benefactor of more peaceful feelings. Self-imposed stress in the form of pride and ego fulfillment doesn't have to happen at all. You can choose a different course. You can opt to take in beautiful moments, rather than striving to create them.

Most stress is harmful because it leads to mental fatigue that negatively affects your performance and health. Stress isn't always a negative, however. It can even be invigorating under the right circumstances. Eustress (good stress) makes you feel more alive. Stress that brings excitement and makes you enthusiastic doesn't put you on a psychiatrist's couch. Stress that gets you off your butt and into your running shoes changes "ho-hum" into "git-er-done."

There's nothing wrong with entering a Miss Universe or Mr. Olympia contest when such endeavors are infrequent, special events that enrich the lives of those who enjoy competition. There is also nothing wrong with striving to do your best, even if it requires some sacrifice in order to showcase what you do well. Once winners have been announced and buffet tables have been put away, blood pressures that were temporarily elevated usually return to normal. The effects of such stresses don't last long, because special events aren't everyday happenings. But life cannot be properly enjoyed if stress is continual. When interactions and aspirations are consistently intense, a person eventually burns out. One's flame needs to stay lit.

Your voice is the puppet of your conscious intent, but what you say does not necessarily equate with your subconscious status. You can utter, "I'm strong," but below the level of consciousness believe, *I'm weak.* You can say, "No problem," but internally have the perception, *That troubles me.* Your desire to put on a good show can portray humility to those around you, even though your ego may be lacking sustenance.

To be accepted socially, you temper many of your statements, especially those that would expose pride. You know you have to be careful about what you project, because you don't want others to perceive you as a threat. The fact that you occasionally must be deceitful in this way doesn't mean that the impulses you are controlling are improper ones. Only blatant proclamations of self-importance are unacceptable, not the mindset of self-importance. There's nothing wrong with believing that your spirit is special, for that spirit is all you are, all you know, all you experience. Your existence is magical, and it's understandable to reason that your uniqueness must serve a special purpose. Every spirit is sacred, and it's essential that you honor yours. You are wrong if you don't place a high importance on yourself.

To be at peace you must feel gratified. The need for gratification is #1. It drives everything you do. In order to be gratified you must acquire what you need, and determine that you are satisfied with those things, things like having shelter and enough food to eat, loving and being loved, and feeling comfortable in your surroundings. Since gratification is your driving force, it's natural to be troubled when your desires don't materialize. Feeling unfulfilled brings stress and heightens one's angst. When you don't experience gratification, you begin to have longings that impel a search for something better. Prolonged, continual searching is troublesome. It evidences a chronic dissatisfaction. Even though you are special and your moments are too few, an exaggerated self-importance makes it tough to reach your expectations. Many people set the bar too high, thereby making it impossible to clear, and resulting in their always passing under it. The more humility you have, the lower that bar has to be and the easier it is to achieve gratification.

It's ironic that when one centers too much on achieving gratification, gratification becomes even more elusive, with a worsening of the very problems that have been interfering with gratification. There are numerous situations where longings cannot be alleviated, and where a choice must be made between continuing to feel bad and finding the humility to cease defining those aspirations as prerequisites for your happiness. The application of inner humility is the easiest way to calm your ego, so that unrealistic desires can evolve into reasonable ones that are more likely to bring gratification. Being humble is one more aspect of self-determination, of taking control of how you feel.

Giving the appearance of being humble will do little for your self-image. You must experience humility. You must believe in the rightness of owning a humbled ego. Contrary to what may seem logical, the tempering of pride actually raises self-esteem because it allows one to feel more adequate. It's up to you to decide if you would rather perform on stage or be in the audience. Does your spirit thrive on stress, or would it prefer to feel at peace?

In the previous chapter, you learned how important it is to look for the simple positives. They become more obvious when you are humble. It's difficult to perceive value in the common place when you define ordinary things as "not worthy of my attention." Please do not allow such arrogance. Instead, increase your humility so that you will become more appreciative of the simple positives, thereby multiplying your blessings.

Being humble doesn't necessitate giving up on or down playing life's important matters. Gaining inner humility is not a sacrifice; it's a gift to yourself. Your attitude becomes more positive as you trade pride for humility. With humility you are the master of your experience, rather than a slave of your ambitions.

The Changeover's definition of humility:
AN EGO AT PEACE.

11

Truth

Throughout the universe and across every dimension, the one fundamental element that is absolutely unyielding is truth. Nothing else is more steadfast, pure, and reliable. It is impossible to refute something that is true. Truth can be hidden or ignored, but it cannot be undone.

Truth is often thought of in the context of a moral code of conduct such as "One should always be truthful." The ramifications of truth in relation to virtue will be forthcoming in the chapter entitled, "Honor." At this time, we will be considering truth as it pertains to your primary perspective.

A primary perspective should arise from accurate personal definitions, but accuracy is difficult to achieve because we are error-prone, emotional beings, not soulless computers. Feelings envelope our thoughts and, as a result, we occasionally make definitions that satisfy our emotional needs without regard for logic or truth. Also, the truth can be frightening. It can't be manipulated like presumptions and fantasies, therefore many people evade it for fear of what they might have to accept. But hiding from truth is no better than living a lie, and lies are in partnership with all the other negatives that are harmful to a perspective.

A perspective is only as dependable as the personal definitions that create it. A perspective containing self-deceit is an unstable one, for whenever such definitions become exposed, not only are any benefits they produced obliterated, but also a shadow is cast on other definitions that are being relied upon.

Your happiness must be secure, not tenuous and susceptible to being revoked. A lie may temporarily help you address a negative emotion, but in the long run, truth is a much better friend.

Truth does not hide, yet it can be difficult to see, even when it surrounds you. That's because you have been indoctrinated with inaccuracies that cloak the truth. These indoctrinations have led to suppositions that are now integral components of your reasoning process. Testing your beliefs to find if they are truthful may be uncomfortable for you, but it is something you need to do, because truth is the most important component of your changeover.

Most of your personal definitions were formed hastily. You grabbed hold of whatever you heard, took what you wanted from it, made your own interpretation, and then entitled that interpretation as "truth" without putting much thought into the process. Sometimes you did a good job of it, but sometimes you just compounded the errors already present in your belief system, now exemplified by an inconsistent point of view or by being noncommittal in some of your beliefs. When you rely on uncertainties, you end up with self-doubt, unsure of who you really are or what you stand for. Unreliable definitions can cause you to feel unprotected and vulnerable to the point where you feel it's safest to close your mind to new information.

Many people don't give sufficient priority to truth because truth isn't critical to them. They deem comfort and conflict avoidance to be more important than complete honesty, hence the socially acceptable "white lie." In primitive societies, truth and survival are inseparable, but in societies where comforts are plentiful, truth can be seen as too noxious or too inconvenient.

People enthusiastically praise the attribute, truthfulness, yet disregard facts that are contrary to their own personal definitions. When beliefs are not supported by truth, there is no substance to back up those beliefs and, therefore, the associated individual perspectives are not reliable.

Those who are in control of their outlook understand that truth is better than delusion. Even though they still occasionally dream, these individuals know that their moments exist in the real world. The truth may not always bring them happiness, but it is something on which they can depend. As a result, their lives are as predictable and secure as they can be. Think how much better off these people are than those who have perspectives that are fragile or lack integrity.

I'm convinced that there are plenty of facts to support any perspective one chooses to have. If you are guided by truth, any road can be a freeway. Whatever your endeavor, you move through life in a bold and straightforward manner when your thoughts and actions are supported by truth.

When making personal definitions, resist the temptation to deceive your perspective. Only use information that truthfully fits your purpose, selecting the most helpful among the available factual options. It's permissible to occasionally color a definition by de-emphasizing facts that would be antagonistic to your goal, but you must be careful not to base too large a portion of your personal definitions on such spins. Occasional, creative interpretations are acceptable when you are building individual perspectives, but don't dilute the basic formula on which everything else is founded by allowing a disproportionate number of half-truths to substantiate your beliefs. Commit to accepting reality. Work with what life has to offer, and strive to make positive interpretations using those facts.

Try to be flexible and receptive to new realizations, and be open-minded when contemplating the validity of your assessments, both old and new. More than a passing glance should be given to all information. Reserve final judgments until you have substantiated your initial impressions. Play the Devil's advocate to test the correctness of your existing beliefs, and be willing to discard any erroneous assumptions as though they were no big deal.

It's inevitable that some of tomorrow's facts will conflict with today's "truths." When this happens, your catalogued definitions may not automatically adjust. They may even resist being changed. You'll then have to decide whether or not you are willing to redefine those beliefs. You can decide to be loyal to your existing definitions, regardless of the new facts, but if that's what you do, you will have effectively made the decision to close the door on your thought process.

There's a tendency to defend one's personal definitions, no matter what the facts, and that can result in more than a bruised ego these days. Why do we so stubbornly protect our antiquated opinions? Is comfort so important that we'd rather accept a falsehood than make a revised definition? The greatest adversary can be one's own inflexibility.

The more value you give to a personal definition, the more protectively you guard it. Just as a special occasion can be awarded a higher-than-normal value, a key personal definition can also be perceived as having an elevated worth. Clinging to valued beliefs that no longer hold up is self-defeating. Be honest with yourself. Be receptive to change when confronted with a conflicting fact. Adhere to the poignant expression, "To thine own self be true."

Even though the truth can be frightening, you shouldn't run from it. Consider this example:

Winston is a thirty-five-year-old husband and father. He has been a heavy smoker since age eighteen. He has not had any serious health concerns until recently, but for the past two weeks he's been experiencing a persistent, hacking cough, difficulty breathing, and periodic chest pains.

Winston knows that a smoking habit greatly increases the risk of developing both lung cancer and heart disease, and that these recent symptoms should be checked by a physician, but he's fearful of what an examination and tests may reveal. Therefore, he elects to define his physical distress as just a stubborn, insignificant cold, and he convinces himself that he has nothing to worry about. Instead of properly investigating his symptoms, he makes his own diagnosis, selecting from the available possibilities a definition that he prefers to believe, one that eases his fears and allows him to perceive a happy ending.

Hopefully Winston has made the right decision. If so, his assessment of the situation will have prevented needless expense and stress, and it will have freed his mind to focus on other concerns. But if he has guessed wrong, he might be missing the only window of opportunity he has for curative treatment. Because he fears being confronted with a negative truth, Winston has created a definition that allays his concerns, but by not making a commitment to discovering the truth, he may have decreased the odds of achieving that happy ending he has envisioned.

Truth cannot be defined away. Your definitions can mask the truth, or influence how you react to it, but they can't change the truth. Truth does not bend to your will. Truth does not yield. Whether a positive or a negative, truth will endure, therefore it must be accepted, even when it is painful. Without exception, when it comes to truth, you can run, but you cannot hide.

Since truth is invincible, from now on accustom yourself to beginning every thought process from a position of truth. Don't waste time trying to hide from negative facts or attempting to spin them into oblivion, especially when your precious moments are at stake. Accept truth as a given in your life. Respect the absolute power it holds. When a truth causes unpleasant feelings, either check the perimeter to see what good might be accompanying that negative truth, or look for positives that could be created from it.

There are times when you won't be able to perceive an associated positive, but even if you can't, it's better to honor truth rather than myth. By honoring truth you'll be honest with yourself and attuned to whatever must be done to make your moments as good as possible, using the cards you've been dealt.

When the truth isn't known or understood, it's quite natural to make suppositions to fill the gaps in your understanding. Your mind doesn't like uncertainty. Whenever the truth is elusive, it's logical that you attempt to eliminate those uncomfortable voids by coming up with personal definitions that are guesses or assumptions. Small errors in your library of definitions are acceptable as long as they contribute to the development of a positive perspective, and as long as they are not made with the knowledge that they are incorrect. Keep in mind, however, that when guesses are substituted for facts, such definitions are tenuous and, at some point, they may need to be reworked.

A supposition is fine as long as you are receptive to re-examining it should it later appear to be wrong. Ancient astronomers contemplated the Earth's relationship to the heavens, and made the logical supposition that the Sun revolved around the Earth. For thousands of years, scientists and philosophers alike held to that belief. What had seemingly been an irrefutable fact has since been proven to be incorrect. Likewise, some of the "truths" that you are now relying upon will be shot down in the future. When that happens, don't let the new findings upset you, just make the necessary corrections to your internal computer, and then move on. Don't be frightened by new information that goes against a key belief or opinion. Truth is not a threat; it's just the way things are. That's how you should look at it. As information changes, your beliefs must adapt. It's acceptable to have an honest belief in something that's unknowingly false, but should you become privy to facts that prove that belief to be incorrect, then adapt your thinking accordingly. Don't hold onto a definition that has proven to be inaccurate. Truth should never be optional.

Honoring truth may occasionally put you in conflict with those who have a limited commitment to it, and also with those who tenaciously cling to their own, inaccurate personal definitions. Anything you do that departs from the beliefs of the collective ego will distinguish you and open the door to prejudice against you. So how will you stay upbeat in a hostile environment? By knowing that you are right! Truth will be your empowerment.

Living in truth makes you aware of the many untruths around you, and the contrast between your interpretations and the misconceptions of others heightens your self-respect. But before you start considering yourself a Moses among the pagans (even though that is what you might be), remember to remain humble, for even at your best, some of your reasoning will be flawed. You will occasionally be as incorrect as those whom you believe to be incorrect. If you are committed to truth, welcome every opportunity to hear opinions that are contrary to yours. Differences in perspective are thought-provoking, and being receptive to new facts is how your mind stays rust-proofed. Remember, there was a time when even the greatest minds believed the Earth was flat.

If you are determined to make the most of your moments, your first act should be making a personal commitment to seek truth. Truth is the essence of your changeover. Dedicate yourself to truth. Make this pledge to yourself: *My perspective will be founded on truth, and I will honor truth, regardless of its message.*

12
Tolerance

When I was in high school, my buddies often joked about a particularly unattractive girl who attended our school. Although I didn't approve, I quietly tolerated their insensitive humor. This was due to my lack of self-confidence in those days. I was more of a follower than a leader, and the role of a follower is to be tolerant of those seeking the spotlight.

Since I was well practiced at tolerating such behavior as a youth, you'd think that as I matured, I would have gained even more tolerance. It was just the opposite. As I grew older, I became increasingly less tolerant of things that annoyed me. I'm not sure why this happened. Perhaps I reached my limit of restraint. Maybe it was because with maturity I became more self-assured, and then reacted more honestly to things that bothered me. Whatever the reason, as I grew older, I became more openly critical and less amenable.

Even though I now enjoy a positively-weighted perspective, hardly a day goes by when I don't struggle to quash my habit of negative criticism. I still have to remind myself to be tolerant of the people and situations that don't conform to how I think things ought to be.

People who can't value their own moments are, understandably, not going to be overly considerate of mine, so for me to live among others and not let them rip my perspective apart, I've had no option but to accept their annoyances as the inconsequential acts they typically are. Instead of allowing a behavior to rattle me, I strive to improve my tolerance of that behavior.

When one person is annoyed by another, it's not always the result of rudeness or an incompatibility. A person can have a primary perspective that is very similar to yours, yet still forget to use his turn signal, or sneeze beside you in an elevator, or walk slowly in front of you when you're in a hurry. From time to time, we all unintentionally bug someone else, and they then have their own tolerance or intolerance to deal with.

We've little control over what other people do, but we are in complete control of how we interpret their actions. Being annoyed by other peoples' behaviors exposes our own prejudices and weaknesses. The majority of the time it's our own shortcomings that are responsible for the aggravation we feel, not the faults of others.

Being annoyed isn't a petty matter. Whenever you proclaim something to be annoying, you're admitting that you've adopted a negative point of view. Since it's not possible to feel simultaneously negative and positive, being intolerant is self-defeating by the sheer loss of your positivism. Oppositely, tolerance dismisses the negative impact that something might otherwise make on you. In order to be positive in a world that tests you each day, it's best to be tolerant, rather than intolerant. Little annoyances add up, and even a small one can instantly change you from being happy to feeling angry.

An immediate, averse reaction to an annoyance is always a preprogrammed response. To instantly perceive something as "annoying," one has to have already defined it as an irritant, and the more that irritant is repeated, the more instantaneous and thoughtless your reaction. Something pulls your trigger and —BAM!— you have a conditioned response, faster than you can think. Not only is this spontaneous reaction the result of pre- programming, but also, the degree to which you're affected is a preset. It's easy to feel instant anger without significant cause.

Your mind doesn't have the time to go through a logical thought process to determine how you'll interpret a sudden, negative stimulus. Instead, you exhibit a knee-jerk, negative response. Wouldn't it be better if that reaction was, instead, a knee-jerk tolerance: an unthinking and immediate, positive response? You can condition yourself to react that way. Just as you have become programmed for automatic intolerance when faced with negative stimuli, you likewise can be programmed for automatic tolerance.

You've been reading that a single act can be interpreted as either a negative, a positive, or anywhere in between, depending on who's doing the interpreting, and the state of mind that individual happens to possess at the time. The interpretation, not the act, is the variable. Every act is a fact, unable to be undone once committed. Your response is what can be shaped. The most constructive way to deal with annoyances that play upon your emotions is to prepare for them in advance8.

When a hurricane is approaching, there's nothing you can do to alter its course. However, you can secure your property and evacuate the area if necessary. With forewarning it's possible to minimize the impact of high winds and flooding. But how do you prepare yourself for something like a lightning bolt, something that strikes abruptly and without warning?

Since it isn't possible to intercept an unpredictability, your best option is to pre-condition yourself to make a quick, constructive response, similar to slamming on your brakes when another car pulls out in front of you. When behind the wheel, you never know when a quick reaction will be needed, but if you're a good, defensive driver, you drive with the anticipation that an evasive maneuver will be required at any moment. Your training, experience, and determination to be safe in your vehicle help you to react without thinking when an unexpected danger suddenly appears.

The attainment of a primary perspective that faces all challenges with a positive expectation provides a substantial degree of automatic tolerance. With a positive mindset, negatives are dulled before they are perceived to be problems. A positive perspective sweetens all perceptions, similar to how putting sugar on freshly cooked rhubarb reduces its pucker potential.

But you can heighten that augmented tolerance further by conditioning yourself to sidestep instantaneous interpretations. Just as you practice defensive driving, you can practice defensive tolerance. You can preprogram yourself to slow your initial reactions to negatives so they won't trigger a split-second, negative response, thereby giving you time to consider the situation more thoughtfully.

Evading a negative reaction equates with counting to ten before allowing your emotions to come into play. A delayed response helps establish neutral ground on which to begin considering how a stimulus will affect you. Once you've blocked an automatic reaction, you can then take charge of what occurs next. By intercepting a negative reflex, you delay the rising of emotions, and you gain time to think, which provides the opportunity to redefine negative perceptions into ones that you can either tolerate or perhaps disregard altogether. When you intercept a negative emotional response, you then can react with calmer thoughts, such as *Hmmm… interesting*, or *Oh well…no problem*, rather than *What a jerk!* or *Not in my lifetime!* The sayings, "Boys will be boys" and "That just goes with the territory" exemplify softened, tolerant responses to negative stimuli.

Work at developing good interceptive reflexes. Quickly apply the brakes when you feel yourself reacting negatively. Defuse the situation. If you feel your face beginning to flush and your emotions beginning to rise, think *Wait a minute!* then switch from an emotional state to an objective one. In no time at all, the repetition of intentional tolerance will become your dominant, conditioned response, replacing the spontaneous, negative reactions that grew from past conditioning.

Most things that bother you are trivialities that bring unwarranted distress. By learning to take the sting out of those minor irritations, you can pass them off as the inconsequentialities they truly are. Eventually you won't react to them at all, because they will no longer be annoyances. That's the power of intentional mental design. As your primary perspective becomes more positive, your negative perceptions will be reduced, and when you become adept at intercepting negative responses, you'll have achieved the ultimate in self-control, making you the master of your emotions.

∗∗∗

Long before science confirmed the existence of balancing positive and negative ions in all matter, the ancient Chinese theorized that there are two counteracting cosmic forces that shape and balance the Universe: Yin and Yang.

After centuries of observation, they concluded that these opposing energies exist to prevent the cosmos from being static. Supposedly, Yin and Yang are in continual states of flux and tension, and at any moment one or the other is dominant. The interplay of these forces brings continual change, yet they ultimately complement one another, resulting in overall harmony. By way of this dynamic relationship, Yin and Yang create life and influence events.

Harmony

Western civilization generally believes "positive" is good and "negative" is bad. The Chinese philosophers saw it differently. Their Yin and Yang were not perceived as either good or bad. They believed them to simply be natural forces, pulling and pushing, with neither one being essentially harmful or beneficial.

Yin and Yang operate somewhat like a railroad hand car, where two people stand at either end of a fulcrum lever, each working oppositely, either pushing down or pulling up on their handles. It would seem that these efforts would cancel each other out, yet that reciprocating motion moves the hand car steadily down the track. Do you see how a belief in balancing forces would instill a perspective that's more accepting of the ups and downs in life? The theory of Yin and Yang promotes a relaxed attitude that's more tolerant than one that perceives life as a battle between good and evil.

Negatives are usually considered to be undesirable, but negatives must exist in one form or another in order for a person to experience positive feelings. Without negatives there can be no positives. In fact, without the interplay of negatives and positives, we'd have no feelings at all, just an eternal sameness.

Any way you choose to look at it, opposing energies do exist, and they are an integral part of your moments. Living isn't positive or negative—it just is what it is. If intelligent beings weren't around to make biased interpretations, there would be no right or wrong, just things happening in balance, moving steadily down the track like a railroad hand car. By adding a sense of Yin and Yang to your perspective, you can lessen the villain status of negatives, bringing you greater peace, and helping you to be more tolerant of those things that you've thus far defined as "negatives."

Although positives and negatives may generally be in harmony with one another, that doesn't mean that huge fluctuations do not occur, it's just that positives and negatives eventually turn around. After reaching the bottom of a crevasse, the only place one can go next is back up. After reaching a pinnacle, the next step has to be down. There would be no "Oh, my throbbing head… I'll never do that again!" on New Year's Day, without there first being a New Year's Eve celebration the night before. No one would ever exclaim, "I'm so relieved!" after receiving good news from a mammogram reading, if there wasn't first the fear of having breast cancer. Often, when experiencing a positive or negative, the opposite perception is just around the corner.

An arrow shot into the sky comes back down due to earth's gravitational pull. You can repeatedly reach the sky by shooting an arrow, then retrieving it, and then shooting it again, but that approach only provides cycles of up-and-down success. However, a solid-fuel rocket with multiple boosters not only can override gravity, it has the potential to take its payload far beyond the solar system. The Yin and Yang of life can be intermittently tolerated by periodic surges of determination, but surges don't provide steady tolerance. It takes more than surges to permanently override the natural order.

There are so many things that can help power you to rise above the ebb and flow that would otherwise play on your emotions. This additional energy can be obtained from motivational lectures, uplifting novels, good music, and heart-to-heart talks with a friend. You can be energized by a funny story, by being around a pet that makes you smile, or simply by getting busy. As your inner resources are consumed, positive influences can be tapped to give you the boosts you need to maintain your tolerance.

Whatever you do, never fuel distress. Apply the brakes when you sense spontaneous negative interpretations. Keep positives flowing by reaching out to every possible resource, and don't wait until your tolerance tank is empty before seeking more fuel, or you may then have to deal with the additional burden of increased anxiety, hostility, and depression. Not only will those negative emotions make you feel even worse, they'll take much more effort to resolve than the effort that would've been expended to keep your tolerance going.

***

There are two types of tolerance: **tolerance-by-acceptance** and **tolerance-by-endurance**. Perceived nuisances that are the result of human behavior can be readily tolerated by accepting the behavior. This tolerance-by-acceptance can be achieved by:

1) Acknowledging that the nuisance is your interpretation.
2) Defining the behavior as being inconsequential to your happiness.

3) Moving your thoughts from the nuisance to something else that's a more beneficial focus.

Tolerance-by-acceptance completely neutralizes negativity, because with acceptance, the negative perception disappears.

There are enumerable irritations that are not related to human behavior, however: frigid temperatures, mosquito bites, sore throats, hunger, etc. These are difficult to define away, because they are physical perceptions rather than psychological ones. Such irritations require tolerance-by-endurance. With tolerance-by endurance, there are two possible outcomes:

1) You endure the difficulty until it passes, or you eventually become resistant to it.
2) You endure the difficulty for a while, but eventually wear down and lose your tolerance.

Tolerance-by-endurance is most effective when a negative stimulus is short-lived. When you must endure a drawn-out negative experience, you can best achieve this tolerance by dividing your problem into smaller time segments, converting it into a series of short-lived events. Having a hiccup or two is no big deal—easy to tolerate—but if you can't stop hiccupping, at some point tolerance ebbs. When confronted with something that's a prolonged distress, what you have to do is narrow your focus to a time frame that is manageable. Just concentrate on making it through the next "hiccup," and continue this tolerance-by-endurance technique until the negative eventually fades.

Some difficulties demand an exceptional level of tolerance. A crisis is one of these events. By definition, a crisis has a limited lifespan. To tolerate a crisis, you first need to step back and look at the bigger picture. This has the effect of immediately tempering the negative perceptions that are being created, especially if you can rationalize that your crisis will eventually evaporate even if no effort is put into it. A crisis is best tolerated by definition adaptations, with the degree of success dependent on your determination to turn things around.

However, when a stressful situation is long-term, tolerance can't be achieved by stepping back and looking at the bigger picture. Doing so might carry you for a while, at least give you time to think things through, but what if nothing ever changes? What about the no-win situations? What about those toughest of times?

When one feels terrible and relief can't be envisioned, pain and stress become projected into infinity, and every bit of positive attitude can disappear. A hopeless view of the future is why people take their own lives. For someone who feels completely defeated, the "bigger picture" can't alleviate their negative thoughts. In fact, it may heighten them. The future contains too much territory and too many unknowns.

The best way to manage such an event, whether psychological or physical, is to again reduce the problem into smaller bits. In other words, focus only on individual pieces of the problem. Just as anyone can eat an entire elephant, one bite at a time, almost any situation can be tolerated when it is converted into smaller perceptions. Not only do you benefit by disassembling an unmanageable experience into its more tolerable components but also you're then able to think more acutely. When your focus is tightened, it's easier to make point definitions that together lessen the weight of the negative perception, and may even lead to an eventual resolution of the problem.

It's not necessary to have the energy today to tolerate a lifetime of stress. No one can maintain their tolerance when negative images are projected that far ahead. The effective place to begin tolerating a mountainous negative is where a measure of control can be exercised, and that's always within the closest perception. Commit to surviving the moment—one week, one hour, one second. Avoid thinking about what you will have to tolerate tomorrow, just tolerate this instance. Adjust your energies to where they'll do the most good. When you concentrate on taking care of "now," you will simultaneously be working on tomorrow, next week, and next year. By having the determination to deal with just this moment, and then adding the necessary positive fuel to sustain your tolerance into only the next moment, you can positively impact the future course of events, even when dealing with a persistent, negative force.

People rarely think of becoming more tolerant as a way to handle their problems, because they see tolerance as coping, not curing. They want their problems to end. But some problems never go away, and some can't have their impact reduced by way of changes to their definitions. A perspective has to remain as healthy as possible in the presence of such problems, and that sometimes be the result of pure determination.

It may seem to be a contradiction, but there are times when intolerance is healthy. Although intolerance adds negative weight to a perspective, it can add even greater positive weight when it precipitates positive action. The reason why people take up causes, such as fighting for their rights, battling against evil, or correcting their faults, is because they are intolerant of things they believe to be destructive. Efforts to defeat something deemed "intolerable," rather than to tolerate it, can bring constructive feelings as well as the potential for positive gains.

Whenever you refuse to surrender to a negative, or even to Yin and Yang, you are being intolerant. If you choose to be less accepting than you could be, you are choosing to be less tolerant. This isn't always bad, because if you were tolerant all the time, you'd find yourself in an amoebic existence. Being selectively intolerant is fine, as long as you're not intolerant to the point where that negativism creates a negative outlook.

It's a breeze to be intolerant, but it takes a certain level of skill to exercise tolerance. Therefore, start working on becoming more tolerant. By increasing your tolerance, you'll have one more tool to help you achieve the best possible perspective, even amid situations that are not conducive to positive thoughts.

13

Patience

Animals are far more patient than humans, because they have less on their minds, less to be anxious about. Can you imagine yourself perched atop a bronze statue throughout the day, waiting for the occasional bread crumb to drop from a passerby's sandwich, or lying for hours on a front porch, waiting patiently for your master to come home from work? It's quite gross (thanks, Discovery Channel), but how about those hungry crocodiles that lie on the riverbank for weeks, just biding their time until the next wildebeest migration?

Americans are among the most anxious of the human population. If there was an annual award given to the nation whose citizens displayed the greatest patience, the United States would likely have an empty trophy case. We're quite good at strength and endurance, but patience? Not our forte! Just think about it: there are few things Americans do that aren't done as expeditiously as possible.

For example, a day of fishing should give hours of relaxation. At least that's how my Grandpa Johnson saw it. He would make the long trip up Big Cottonwood Canyon, hike from the road to his favorite stream, and then peacefully fly-fish all day long, happy to return home with just two or three nice trout. So, what's with the fisherman who puts two hundred horsepower on the transom of an eighteen-foot, metal flake surfboard, so he can race to cover miles of shoreline in just a few hours? This certainly doesn't exemplify patience.

Here are some interesting opposites:

Patience...Impatience

On foot...On board

Country lane...Superhighway

Ford Model-T...Porsche 911

Queen Mary..Airbus

Campfire..Bottled gas

Oven-baked...Microwaved

Pad & pencil...i-Pad

Postal Service...E-mail

Four dates, one kiss...........One date, "My place or yours?"

Why are we so impatient? Is patience something we've forgotten, or could it be that Americans have never been patient? Whatever the answer, it appears that the contemporary thinking is, *"I don't have time to be patient."*

The capacities to be both patient and tolerant are valuable traits. As with appreciation, patience and tolerance promote consistently good, day-to-day feelings. Both patience and tolerance help us to be accepting and to remain calm. Here's how they differ:

Tolerance is associated solely with negative perceptions, whereas patience can relate to both negatives and positives.

Tolerance relates to something that is happening now, whereas patience involves something yet to happen.

Patience

Tolerance

Intelligent thinking involves perusing all realms of time. You look ahead, look back, and study what's happening right in front of you. Your mind doesn't like being confined to a specific moment. It loves to move across the timelines, scanning all relevant information pertaining to whatever happens to be its interest.

Even though you may attempt to limit your focus to a single past, present, or future event, you can't shut out the other time frames that continually live within your peripheral vision, ready to be drawn to the forefront by the slightest catalyst. You are never more than a millisecond away from being pulled into dimensions where emotions play against logic.

When you allow your mind to spend a significant amount of time considering future possibilities, whether good or bad, you are bound to acquire anxious feelings. It's easy to be consumed by unwarranted anxiety. However, even bona fide stresses can be countered by exercising patience.

It follows that if patience is an asset, then being impatient is a liability. If you think about it, being impatient reveals that you are dissatisfied with the moment, and that you crave another moment to replace the one that you're in. Even trying to make your life the best it can be may reveal impatience. Appreciating the moment necessitates being in the moment, rather than wishing it away or longing for something anticipated.

Impatience is a one-hundred-percent negative characteristic, and you are one-hundred-percent responsible for it. It's self-defeating to be impatient. Impatience always detracts from the moment, because appreciation can't coexist with impatience. Most of the time, impatient feelings are subtle and cause little harm, but if impatience is your nature, your habitual way of going from moment to moment, those subtleties are hurting you. There is no question that you are better off, both emotionally and physically, when you exercise patience.

Here's another short assignment. See if you can match each of the following impatient statements with its less-stressful alternative:

THE TWELVE *IMPATIENT* MOMENTS OF CHRISTMAS:

1) "How many days until Christmas, Daddy?"
2) "I'm going crazy wondering if he got my hint."
3) "I can't wait to see the look on her face!"
4) "Let's go to bed early so that tomorrow comes faster."
5) "Just a little more assembly, and then I'll be able to relax."
6) "Mommy! Daddy! Please wake up!"
7) "Why do we have to eat breakfast first?"
8) "These slippers are a boring gift. I wonder what's in that other box?"
9) "Don't play with it now, Chris. Hurry up…you have more gifts to open."
10) "Two more hours until kick-off, then it'll be my turn to have fun."
11) "When the kids are done, I'll finally be able to give her my special gift."
12) "As soon as we finish Christmas dinner, let's plan our New Year's Eve party."

THE TWELVE *PATIENT* MOMENTS OF CHRISTMAS:

A)   "I plan to enjoy the entire day."
B)   "There's no hurry. We'll save the other presents and you can open them later."
C)   "I love her face."
D)   "I'm so glad the kids are having a great time."
E)   "Christmas will be here before you know it."
F)   "Regardless of what gifts I'm receiving, this moment is fun."
G)   "After dinner, before we do anything else, let's sit together and savor the Christmas spirit."
H)   "I see Santa left a present for Jona, one for Erin, one for me…"
I)   "Christmas Eve is the best night of the year."
J)   "I know I'll love whatever he gets for me."
K)   "Let's first have a special breakfast to begin this special day."
L)   "It's really fun being Santa's elf."

(Matchups at the end of this chapter)

The purpose of these comparisons is to demonstrate that you can be impatient and not even realize it. Impatient thoughts like those described are quite innocuous, but they nonetheless take away from the moment at hand. This type of impatience and the stress associated with it can affect you all year long, often subtly, yet still adding up. Every time you allow yourself to be impatient, you are demon starting a focus on a non-reality, rather than the true moment. This undermines your living experience. Being impatient is always self-defeating.

Patience is an offshoot of a perspective that respects time and truth. When a perspective prioritizes the moment, the future becomes less important, resulting in a more peaceful state of mind. When time becomes less of a factor, time slows down and life becomes more fulfilling. Since your time is so precious, wouldn't you rather have it decelerate than to have it speed up? Being patient is self-rewarding, rather than self-defeating. Strive for it. Don't wish away your moments!

Remind yourself to take interceptive action whenever you feel impatient. Become more patient by prioritizing what is happening now. Refuse to be anxious.

It doesn't matter whether you gain patience or eliminate impatience; it ends up the same. But if one approach seems to stall, try the other. Follow the thought process that works best for you. Whatever you do, do not allow the unknown to dictate how you feel. Deal with the facts as they come to light, so you can respond to them in the best possible way. Time spent in an anxious, impatient state of mind, no matter how briefly, adds negatives to your perspective.

Patience relates to living, whereas impatience relates to fantasy or speculation. The present moment is your truth. When you are patient, you are feeling that truth. The next time you are impatient, use that anxious feeling to remind yourself that your view of life has slipped out of focus. End that feeling by returning your thoughts to a more beneficial, patient perception.

(Impatient/Patient Matchups: 1-E, 2-J, 3-C, 4-I, 5-L, 6-H, 7-K, 8-F, 9-B, 10-A, 11-D, 12-G)

14

Optimism

Through personal definitions you have the power to create positives from scratch. All you have to do to improve the scenes in your life is throw a few switches in your brain. So, does that mean that wearing burlap can be perceived to be as comfortable as wearing silk? In other words, can a personal definition change a perception into something other than what it is?

You have been reading that you should:

1) Perceive things in the best possible light.
2) Create positive personal definitions.
3) Build a positive primary perspective.
4) Give less significance to negatives.
5) Be appreciative, tolerant, and patient.

These suggestions sound like they belong in an optimist's credo, don't they. Does that mean that you should add: "become an optimist" to your list of personal objectives? Is having strong optimism a prerequisite for obtaining an Ultimate Perspective?

A true optimist doesn't look for positives, he expects them. A true optimist doesn't make a determination to have good results; he can't envision things happening any other way. A true optimist is someone whose mind is not in the real world, because his personal definitions contain fantasies.

For ninety-nine percent of the human race, merely choosing to be positive isn't enough, because such an effort won't stand the test of time, nor will it hold up to a barrage of calamities. But, just as there are those who are completely convinced that imagined things really happen to them, some people wholly believe that life is fair, and that good thoughts will insure good results. This book is not written for those who seek impossibilities. The readers I'm trying to help are the ninety-nine percent who fit the same behavioral pattern as I: those who must continually work at being strong and on top of their game.

It's clear that a positive life perspective can only be sustained when founded on truth. Is it possible to be an optimist and still honor truth? If so, the process would be something like: "Build an honest, sustainable optimism by finding truths that support an optimistic view of life." If this could be accomplished, the outcome would result in a natural ease in finding and experiencing positives, thus making it easier to stay courageous and committed to your quest for a positive life experience. How about it? Could you do this?

When you search for positives, you find them. Positives abound. They exist during good times, dull times, and even negative times. You have every reason to expect that, in general, good things will happen to you. What makes optimism not as sound as it might otherwise be is that optimism relates to expectation, and we know that the future can only be presumed, not guaranteed. Therefore, unlike a perspective that's based on positive realities, an optimistic perspective can't be relied upon. An optimistic perspective is based on hope, rather than substance. Although it's easy to discover facts to support honest, positive interpretations, it's not possible to find truths that will insure the fruition of an expectation. Rather than being an attitude born of reality, optimism is an attitude based on wishful thinking or, at best, on favorable odds.

Life isn't always fair, even if one follows the so-called "rules." Life is Yin/Yang unpredictable. The only things over which you have complete control are your personal definitions and your perspectives. You can't control those things that are impossible to control. By being intelligent and by wisely setting your goals, you can influence the course of events, but there are other people in the world who are also trying to manipulate their fates, each one on a different journey, and some pursuing goals that are in direct conflict with your own.

An individual with blind optimism sets himself up for many disappointments, and optimism without supportive facts is a false pretense. I've heard that optimists claim they are more realistic and willing to accept bad news. Such a statement doesn't surprise me, for it's typical of an optimist's mindset of wishful thinking. I believe true optimists wear blinders and rely on positive imaginations, rather than positive realities. Pure optimists are certainly not realists, and they actually have more difficulty accepting bad news, because negative happenings are contrary to their positive expectations. The positive person who bases his perspective on truth-in-reality is the one who is more realistic and best able to deal with negativity.

"Being an optimist" is self-deceit, but "having optimism" is a virtue. This may sound like a contradiction, but it isn't. Realists who subscribe to the premise that most problems can be effectively handled have every reason to have optimism. Such individuals know that life is unpredictable, but they have a justifiable belief that things should eventually work out. This optimistic "color" to their positive perspectives allows them to worry less about the outcome of events, therefore they have less anxiety. A pattern of successful, positive experiences promotes sensible optimism.

The best optimistic posture for you to adopt is to believe that the future holds promise and that you are capable of making the best of whatever comes your way. An intelligent optimism is not being blind to the problems that confront you; it is having the belief that inevitable difficulties will be made better by the skills that you have. In other words, the optimism you should adopt is a belief in yourself and what you are able to do.

Having a reasonable expectation that each day has something good to offer creates enthusiasm for living. Having that kind of optimism gives an individual cause to be excited about the future. Combine optimistic logic with a positive primary perspective, and their symbiotic energies result in an ever-increasing sense of well-being, which is another cycle to perpetuate a positive mindset.

An Ultimate Perspective promotes a positive expectation, and that optimism is deserved because it is factually supported. You don't have to make unrealistic personal definitions in order to have an optimistic perspective. You can keep it real. You can be optimistic without having to believe that burlap feels as fine as silk.

PART II: ENLIGHTENMENT

15
Goals

Your most obvious incentive for setting goals is to improve your quality of life. You also set goals for the pure sake of accomplishment, so that you can augment your self-esteem and prove your worth to others, especially those who have high expectations of you. You may not think of yourself as being goal-minded, but indeed you are. Any wish or hope is a goal, even if you don't see it as one. Passively or actively, you are continually setting goals.

People who merely hope that their desires will someday be satisfied achieve their goals by taking advantage of whatever opportunities happen to come along. Rather than actively working on their goals, these passive goal seekers rely on fate and the efforts of other people to provide them with favorable circumstances. Passive goal setters are opportunists.

Passive goal setters generally prefer to be taken care of, rather than having to expend the energy necessary to be self-reliant. Because of this, it's rare for them to feel fulfilled. Moments are more appreciated if one prioritizes the goal of feeling good, and then does something to achieve that feeling. Complete fulfillment doesn't happen by passively waiting for life to unfold. By doing nothing to affect your course, you become like flotsam drifting the ocean currents, a servant of Yin and Yang. First you experience something nice, then something not so nice.

The complete opposite of passive goal setters are aggressive goal setters: those who willingly self-sacrifice for the sake of achievement. Rather than waiting in line to receive good fortune, the aggressive types take charge of their fate. For them it's, "Look out, here I come!"

Aggressive goal setters take action and get things done, but accomplishments and accolades mean very little if one can't enjoy living, itself. It's difficult to achieve fulfillment when goal seeking is so intense that one suffers because of it. Unless the achievement process creates good feelings, a goal does little to improve one's quality of life. In fact, excessive goal seeking can ruin a life.

Obsessive goal seekers are rarely content, because their rewards exist in the future. Their energies are channeled toward the eventual acquisition of happiness instead of toward being happy now. Wishing upon a star may seem romantic, but making wishes indicates something's lacking. Obsessive goal-seeking behavior is symptomatic of an underlying psychological problem that's being masked, rather than dealt with. These workaholics can't find happiness within their reality, and their heightened ambition— often at the expense of others—is how they escape existences that fall short of their expectations. Goal achievement builds self-image and brings rewards, but if you can't feel satisfied until a goal process has been successfully completed, then the time prior to that accomplishment will be a time of distress.

Those who only dream of success experience very little of it. Those who pursue success relentlessly achieve it, but at a steep price. Complete emotional satisfaction eludes both the passive and the aggressive goal setters. A chronic failure to find happiness in the moment can even cause the abandonment of goals altogether. As in most instances, there's a balance point between the extremes wherein lies the greatest potential for happiness. It's best to set sensible goals and to make a sensible effort, so that you will achieve a higher quality of life without sacrificing the moment.

Goals bring change, and change is stimulating. Your mind thrives on new thoughts and experiences. If a perfect day were repeated time and time again, the perfection of that day would be lost. Change keeps the moment interesting. Change makes you more alert. The best goals are those that create such perceptions.

A small goal that would have seemed insignificant to you in the past might be all you now need to achieve a renewed sense of interest, because you are now developing a perspective that heightens your awareness. How awesome! You don't have to take drastic measures to commence a new direction in your life; just take advantage of opportunities that you've been overlooking. Constructive feelings can come from something as simple as looking for a new road to travel, planning a weekend trip, studying a new subject, or working to perfect an exotic recipe. Whenever you experience change you develop new thoughts, and new thoughts lead to ideas that bring additional changes: yet another beneficial cycle working for you.

Before selecting a goal, consider if the process will or will not be enjoyable for you. Don't set the goal of refinishing a large piece of furniture if you dislike stripping, gluing, and sanding. A goal should be perceived as more than just a desired ending. It should be a stimulating process. If the only purpose of reading a book was to find out how it ends, you would only need to read the last one or two pages. If the only purpose of eating at a fine restaurant was to become full, you could accomplish the same result, and save a lot of money, by staying home and eating a bag of pork rinds. A hundred years of positive life experience is way more meaningful than a one-hundredth birthday.

When the moments spent pursuing a goal are appraised, their perceived value should meet or exceed that of the goal itself. If that can be your criterion, then even if you fall short of your goal, you will at least have been rewarded for the journey—no moments wasted. If you must self-sacrifice and experience steady negative stress in order to accomplish a goal, the benefit of that goal will most likely be negated. You may gamble that you'll be compensated for your sacrifices by eventually hitting the jackpot, but believe me, the odds are not in your favor. If you are betting that a certain accomplishment will make a big difference in your life, when the real problem rests between your ears, then you might as well throw your chips away. Goals bring structure, they are stimulating, and they can be a great adventure, but if a goal process entails sacrifices that will hurt you and/or your family, then you need to thoughtfully reexamine the merits of such a goal.

A questionable goal that has a potential to create negative stress throughout the process can sometimes be made fundamentally sound through creative manipulation. A distress-maker can be converted into a positive force by doing such things as getting your family involved in the goal, or by planning mini-celebrations throughout the process to reward yourself each time you achieve a portion of that goal. If a goal is important enough that the end justifies the means, and, therefore, you choose to proceed regardless of the sacrifice, then find ways to minimize that sacrifice and to compensate for it so that your moments retain a net positive weight.

Take a critical look at the goals on which you have been working and determine if there are other goals that would better serve you. With every proposed goal, ask yourself, *If I fail to achieve it, will I regret having made the effort?* If the answer is *Yes*, or even *Maybe*, then that goal is a hazard to be reconsidered. Don't sacrifice reality for a dream. Don't wager your precious life on something with no guarantee. It's impossible to fully appreciate an accomplishment when an underlying negative attitude exists. Achieving a healthy perspective needs to be #1. The pursuit of any other ambition should be delayed until the goal of achieving a positive mindset has first been achieved. When you have accomplished this, and you then resume working on goals that you temporarily tabled, do so with enthusiasm, and do everything you can to succeed. A goal will not detract from your moments if envisioning its realization makes you feel good, and you then spread that positive attitude throughout your perceptions.

If or when you feel dissatisfied, "feeling better now" is the goal that should supersede all others, not "feeling better eventually." Avoid seeking refuge in superficial goals that only serve to mask a negative state of mind. The longer you allow negativity to consume you, the less likely you will succeed with *any* goal. You may reach a few of them, and you may receive a temporary uplift by each achievement, but the long-term comfort that you need will never result. Whenever your spirit is ebbing, focus on only one goal: turning things around. All your energy, even though you may have very little of it, must be directed specifically toward making changes that will directly affect the source of your unhappiness and your negative perception of it.

The more effort one puts into achieving something in the future, the more difficult it is to appreciate the moment. Goals are extremely beneficial when they make your life better and improve how you feel, but be careful not to make the mistake of trading the living you can do today for something that may never come to pass. Always keep in mind that to be worthwhile, dreams don't have to come true. Dreams have a higher purpose, because even impossible ones are valuable if they stimulate you, provide hope, and add purpose to your moments. Set goals and reap whatever rewards you can, but never lose site of the moment, for the moment is your existence.

16

Health

Generally speaking, he was a sensible man, not a hypochondriac at all, but for whatever reason, probably zest for life, my father was obsessed with his health. He practiced a preventive lifestyle, and to further ensure that he was doing all that he could to develop a resistance to disease, he began each morning with a handful of vitamins and herbal supplements.

My father led a clean life, but he had a mean disposition. His parents must have been excessively cruel to him when he was a child, for he regularly abused my sister and me when we were growing up. Each day he would demand that our horrified taste buds endure cod liver oil, wheat germ, and other nasty substances. Dad always claimed he did it because he loved us, but if he cared so much, why did he chuckle so sadistically as we choked and gagged?

I don't recall my mother taking any of his potions. My father didn't make the same demands of her. I guess she outranked him. She did bring up the subject every now and then, however. I remember hearing her complaining that Dad's garlic capsules and cod liver oil were making him smell like an Italian fisherman, and several times she even threatened to make him sleep in the barn unless he stopped taking "those dang pills." Maybe that's why he spent so much time working outdoors, and maybe that's why their marriage ultimately ended in divorce.

Dad was the hardest worker I've ever known. To me as a child, the physically fit, ex-Navy boxer was as strong as Paul Bunyan and as smart as Thomas Edison. He had the swagger of John Wayne and the bravado of Clark Gable. Being a college professor with a Ph.D. in engineering was not sufficient stimulation for my father; he always had many irons in the fire. Every minute was spent either on his teaching duties or farming his one hundred thirty-five acres. His weekends and evenings were typically dedicated to beans, corn, wheat, or fruit trees. Our orchard, with its need for summer spraying, fall harvest, winter pruning, and spring fertilization was especially time-consuming, permitting no idleness and no time for play.

Year-round, seven days a week, Dad worked from morning until bedtime. Even after fall harvest he would rarely take a break. Instead of spending evenings relaxing with his family, he would stay up late, seated at our kitchen table grading students' papers and preparing for the next day's classes. On weekends, when there were no classes to teach and nothing crop-related to do, there was the never-ending repair and servicing of the farm machinery.

Dad died of brain cancer at age 62. Despite his efforts to stay healthy and live a long life, his time was cut short. He had no family history of cancer, was a teetotaler and non-smoker, and his parents lived with excellent health into their mid-eighties. My mother was certain that his cancer was caused by an excessive consumption of cod liver oil.

Like my father, my wife and I try to keep healthy and to fight the aging process. Not long ago I grew tired of the battle to control my waistline, and I suggested that we consider gracefully accepting the fact that our bodies were changing for the worse. My mate looked at me sternly and exclaimed, "Not me! I'm going out kicking and screaming!" Needless to say, she's the inspiration that keeps me working-out and eating healthily.

Many patients believe that medicines can work magic and that doctors have the ability to cure diseases as easily and as assuredly as a good mechanic can service an automobile. That isn't so—at least not yet. Throughout history, the healing arts have been primarily relegated to assisting the body to repair itself. That's where the greatest success has been achieved. A healthy body heals most minor injuries and ailments within seven to ten days without intervention. This accounts for why a medical doctor, chiropractor, and holistic therapist can have similar success in the treatment of minor physical distress. By the time any course of treatment has ended, the body has had sufficient time to heal itself. Of course, the body can't resolve every infection on its own, or expel cancerous growths, or perform its own implants or transplants, but when it comes to handling routine ills, it does a pretty good job most of the time.

A great deal of outpatient doctoring, therefore, revolves around palliative treatment. Even in a hospital setting, the ultimate magic is within the patient. Sure, in a hospital we can receive medications and replenishing fluids to help our injured bodies do what they are unable to do for themselves, but we are the ones who must repair our damaged tissues. This is why it's so important that we take care of our bodies. It's one of our greatest responsibilities. Being physically fit prepares us to fight the health calamities that inevitably will befall us.

My father bet his chips on what he thought was a healthy lifestyle, but as it turned out, he might as well have been betting on horses. Does that mean he should never have tried? Does his failure indicate the futility of attempting to control fate? You cannot dictate what your health will be. My father was an excellent example of this. You can aid and assist it, you can tweak things here and there, but you are far from having absolute control over it. This is a serious dilemma for someone who wants to maintain an Ultimate Perspective, since staying positive requires feeling good, and being ill puts a strain on even the strongest positive resolve. The more aches and pains one has, the more attention they draw, and the more those discomforts become the focus of the moment.

Your mental and physical fitness are intertwining components. They work to either augment or to detract from your total health, depending on the condition each is in. Both must be sound in order to maximize your sense of well-being. You cannot control every aspect of your health, but you have complete control over your fitness. It is entirely your responsibility.

You must be both mentally and physically in shape in order to function at your best. If either one is in poor condition, the other suffers. My father was physically fit, but mentally out of shape. I believe his Type-A personality, bottled-up emotions, and inability to be at peace contributed to his untimely death. Putting all his efforts into nourishing his body left half the job undone. His cells were nurtured, but his soul was starved.

Your brain is unique in that it has a dual duty. It is the control center for both mental and physical functioning. Because it's a single organ performing multiple tasks, the voluntary and involuntary workings interplay with one another. For example, when you're confronted with danger, your conscious brain interprets the need to act, which triggers the automatic release of adrenaline into the bloodstream. That physical response then makes you more consciously alert, as well as enabling your body to react more quickly. Your heart rate instantly skyrockets, muscles are readied for action, and you obtain a heightened awareness that makes everything seem as though it's happening in slow motion. In this excited state, biological and cognitive functioning are both augmented.

After a perceived danger passes, the adrenaline that you produced leaves you wide-eyed and alert for a while, but after this fight-or-flight response has run its course, stressed muscles become fatigued, and their build-up of pain-causing lactic acid lets your body know that some recuperation time is in order. What begins as mental and physical stimulation ends up as mental and physical let down.

The mind's ability to affect one's vital processes gives it many powers, including the power to heal and the power to shut down. Faith healing is a good example of the mind's constructive power. An ailing person can be touched by a faith healer and experience what would seem to be a miraculous physical recovery, not through the wizardry of the healer, but by the magic of the afflicter's own positive expectation. It's been proven that people who are sick heal more quickly when turning to positive mental activities, such as reading a motivational book, being in the company of pets, or watching humorous films like those by The Three Stooges or Marx Brothers. It is clear that positive thoughts are a boon to one's physical well-being. On the other hand, people who are depressed have been found to be more susceptible to infections and physical deterioration. When the mind gives up the will to live, the body tends to oblige.

I read that people who regularly attend church live an average of six years longer than those who do not. To properly evaluate that statistic, one needs to consider all the variables, including the possibility that lifestyles and habits significantly differ between people who go to church and those who do not. Personally, I don't think God rewards the faithful with a few extra years of life. After all, six years is insignificant when eternity is one's time frame. I attribute this finding to two things: the obvious being that for church-goers, the experience of worshiping provides a health-promoting, positive energy; the less obvious being the probability that those who already feel secure, are at peace, and have good physical and mental health, are more likely to reinforce those positive feelings by attending church than a person who is depressed and does not feel good. Both theories correlate with this chapter's central message, which is:

Good Health Accompanies a Good Perspective.

I used to have extreme difficulty remembering the names of people and places. I am sure this was due to a confused mind, burdened with insecurities and other garbage. I would be introduced to someone, and within ten seconds (no exaggeration) I would not have a clue what name I had been told. This inadequacy resulted in a particularly embarrassing moment for me back in high school. After my freshman year, my girlfriend, Linda, moved to a new home several counties away. She returned some months later for a visit, where she appeared at our local teen hall, a place to dance and hang out on Friday nights. Linda and I were so glad to see each other again that we were inseparable from the time she arrived. A transfer student who had never met Linda came up to us on the dance floor between songs and said, "Hey Lyle, who's your cute friend?" I immediately responded, "Dick, this is…" Yikes! I could not come up with Linda's name. MY FAVORITE PERSON IN THE WORLD! I quickly tried reaching into my mental archives for the precious word that would save me, but the doors were locked shut. After far too many uncomfortable seconds, Linda gave me one of those "looks," and then growled through clenched teeth, "It's Linda!" I was so humiliated! I should have immediately apologized to Linda, but I was so caught off guard that I said nothing at all. My thoughts were solely on myself and my own embarrassment. In fact, I couldn't recover, and the romantic flame that we had been enjoying quickly cooled to an ember. What a jerk I was! Now, decades later, I'm able to think beyond that juvenile self-interest, and I realize how much I must have hurt Linda's feelings that night. I feel sorry for her and for all the others who had to suffer through my growing pains.

Even though I matured over time, my ability to remember names and places remained an embarrassment—that is until my perspective changeover. With my new perspective I became less stressed, and with it my mind became more proficient. I credit this improvement to the elimination of emotional clutter that once competed for my attention. The achievement of a better memory lets me know my mind is now in a better state of health.

But even a perfect Ultimate Perspective cannot directly strengthen muscles or keep arteries clear. For optimum health, the body must also be tuned. A physically fit body is better at handling diseases and injuries than one that is weak and out of shape. Also, a good physical condition contributes to a healthy mindset.

The invigoration that you receive from exercise improves how you feel, but when you don't feel good to begin with, you are not likely to exercise. So, how do you begin? Since you cannot be kick-started with a shot of stimulating endorphins, begin by exercising your mindset, because that's something you can do while sitting on your couch. To get your body moving, first redefine the negative perceptions that are standing in the way, so that you perceive fitness as an enjoyable endeavor, rather than a drudgery. Visualize the benefits you will receive, and begin defining your workout as something to enjoy each day.

Your efforts to be healthy need to be positive in all aspects and, as with any goal, that includes being able to enjoy the process. If exercise is too strenuous or if a diet is too restrictive, you won't be happy and your efforts will not last. If you can enjoy jogging on a treadmill for twenty minutes and then lift weights for another forty minutes, good for you. But, if that is beyond your definition of a positive experience, do whatever works for you, do it regularly, and don't feel guilty or ashamed that you are not doing more. A brisk, or even a slow, ten-minute walk is better than doing nothing, and consistent, light exercise will lead to eventually doing more. The key is doing something regularly, so that it becomes a habit. You don't have to be an exercise fanatic or develop a perfect six-pack in order to feel better than you do now. Any exercise will enhance the way you feel, and that's what's important.

Exercising shouldn't require sacrifice. Sacrifice promotes unhappiness. It's much better that you be a happy hulk than an insipid ideal. If you feel you must make sacrifices in order to maintain or improve your health, work first on improving your perceptions, then begin with exercise that's comfortable and reasonable. Find positives in what you are doing and be patient. A step forward initiates any accomplishment, so start anywhere as long as you start somewhere. Then continue doing whatever it takes to keep you going. Make a conservative plan that will set your goal in motion, and make sure that your goal is reasonable enough to ensure your success. Don't set yourself up for failure by selecting a goal or time frame that's impossible to achieve, and make sure you pursue your goal in a way that's stimulating rather than frustrating. With the right attitude, you can stop smoking, lose weight, or grow washboard abs. Every improvement that you make will help you feel better, and as you feel better you will have the motivation to do more.

In a culture where people strive for excellence in all things, beauty is among those things coveted. But a beautiful face and body is an abnormality. Just look around you. It makes no sense to degrade yourself when, in truth, you fit in very nicely with the rest of the crowd. The distance that one must travel to reach even near-perfection, either physically or intellectually, is much too far for most to reach. This can be disheartening, especially if you have a negative self-image, feel tired much of the time, or are not as healthy as you'd like to be.

However, the inability to achieve perfection doesn't mean you can't make the most of what you have to work with. Don't try to accomplish something that's impossible, and don't strive to achieve an imaginary status. Just do it for yourself. Be happy achieving minor improvements over time. If you find you can't improve, be happy maintaining what you have. Be reasonable in your expectations, and have a good attitude about who you are and what you're doing. With persistence, you will be rewarded. Realize that any improvement to your physical wellbeing is a step in the right direction. Weighing two-sixty is better than weighing two-seventy.

Above all, enjoy the process. That's what it takes to be successful. Build a healthier state of mind, and begin working at becoming more physically fit. As you improve your total health, you will augment both your outward and your inner beauty.

17

Faith

The quest for positives, directly or indirectly, is the supreme motivation for every life form, whether it's the greatest whale or the tiniest microbe. For creatures with an intellect, the acquisition of these positives results in good feelings. The significance of this to you is that your strongest cerebral motivations are linked to your feelings more than to your intellectualizations.

Human feelings are the result of a very complex system of perceptions. These emotions are usually the result of interpretations, which are subjective definitions that may not be factually based. That means a person's preferred state of being, being happy, is not necessarily dependent on truth. As a matter of fact, for many people, distortions of the truth are more comforting than the clarity of reality. Your mind determines your interpretations, and whenever it has a need for positive feelings, your mind has the ability to create them by making positive definitions. If you are sufficiently motivated, you can truly believe whatever you want, regardless of the facts in front of you. But as you have learned, an Ultimate Perspective is founded on truth, so in this chapter we are going to spend a little time making sense out of a situation that has the potential to conflict with your changeover: *Sometimes your feelings would benefit by a certain definition, but you aren't able to determine if the supporting data for that definition is valid.*

What then? Truth is essential for sustaining a healthy perspective, for providing a sound basis for optimistic expectations, and for bringing consistency to those good feelings. Your perspective requires veracity before anything predictable can emanate from it. Even though your personal definitions are subjective in nature, they need to be accurate. But the unadulterated truth can be elusive. What happens when it isn't known? Does the absence of verifying facts prevent you from embracing a belief that, if accepted, has the power to benefit how you feel?

You've been reading that if you can't find factual support for a belief, you should reconsider that belief. However, when there are insufficient facts to steer you one way or the other, and when embracing a specific belief would make a positive contribution to your perspective, it's then acceptable to adopt such a belief on faith.

Whereas truth is bold, faith is subtle. Whereas truth is either black or white, faith is gray. Truth is an attention-getter, an element that produces a dependable effect. Faith is a quiet element, a peaceful repose that replaces contemplative turmoil. Faith alleviates concerns that are too nebulous to be labeled either "black" or "white."

Faith improves how you feel by filling the gaps between the known and the unknown. Faith helps you believe in yourself, and it gives you the confidence to take on new challenges. Faith is an affirmation of the rightness of your discoveries and personal definitions. Through faith, your presumptions become convictions.

Faith is the culmination of your best efforts. Faith is stepping back, looking over the information you have accumulated, and then thinking, *This is what I believe.* When your individual perspectives are founded on solid truth, you have every reason to have faith that your Ultimate Perspective is what it should be. As well as being a testament to your personal definitions, faith is an assuring force that gives you the courage and optimism to apply those beliefs.

Faith is thought simplification. With faith in your perspective, you needn't reconsider all the pieces that make up your point of view every time you use it. It takes a significant amount of contemplation to achieve a perspective changeover, but once you reach the point where your interpretations create a strong and deserved faith, your mind can relax, and you can then turn to a more feeling existence. Instead of having to concentrate on personal definitions and perspective analysis all the time, faith ultimately becomes your guide. Faith allows many of your questions to be assigned to a subconscious mechanism for resolution, which then frees your conscious mind to absorb life without having to continually analyze it.

Faith is an instrument that assists you in making decisions and setting expectations. The mysterious future can be dealt with more positively through the power of faith. Without faith, life contains more uncertainty, which results in a less secure primary perspective. Instead of being restricted by guesses, faith allows you to presume what will be. A presumption is not as dependable a guide as a fact, but when there's no other option, it's better for you to act on faith rather than to have no guidance at all.

A presumption is something that is believed to be true without being proved. Faith that's the result of a presumption is only as reliable as the information that creates the presumption. If you aren't confident in your information, your faith will be weak. If your faith is weak, there's probably something false hidden within it, and the decisions you make on faith will be suspect.

Ask yourself, *Do I have faith in my perspective?* If the answer is a definite *Yes*, you can rely on that good faith belief to logically presume that your vision is twenty/twenty. If you are not confident in your perspective, or if you lack faith in yourself, then your perspective still needs work, because a strong primary perspective should exude faith. Your perspective mirrors the essence of who you are. When your perspective is founded on truth, it is deserving of your faith, which equates to having faith in yourself.

A discussion of faith would not be complete without considering the ramifications of "blind faith." Faith that arises out of logic and truth is credible, whereas blind faith lacks credibility because it has absolutely no supportive substance. If you feel a need to believe in something, but the facts that would encourage that belief don't exist, or you don't care to confirm or prove its veracity, blind faith is your only recourse (obviously a weak one). Be wary of faith that only arises from wishes, for without some validity to support it, you are susceptible to being disappointed, even hurt.

A "good faith belief" is the product of significant personal forethought, whereas "blind faith" is often a dictate of the collective ego. That doesn't mean, however, that a blind faith belief is necessarily incorrect, it just warrants caution. The greater the number of people who espouse a common belief, the more generalized and diluted its supportive facts. If you accept something on faith because someone else says it's what you should do, or because you feel an obligation to support someone else's conviction, keep an open mind about the topic, and look for corroborating information that will allow you to eventually turn that blind faith into a good faith belief.

There's merit in occasionally manipulating the facts, as long as it's a rare occurrence that helps you accomplish your goal of achieving happiness. If all else fails, "whatever it takes" can be an acceptable, last resort. If having a certain belief is essential for your happiness, then believe in it. There are no restrictions on faith as long as your happiness truly benefits from having it. However, faith should never be the mainstay of your belief system. Proven truths must always dominate.

False beliefs often crumble, and when they do, the negative feelings that result are more intense than the initial perceived benefit. Disillusionment is one of the hardest things to accept. One must have exceptional redefining skills in order to overcome a breach of faith, and sometimes nothing will help. When faith is shattered, disappointment, resentment, and anger may have to run their course before the matter can be put aside. The stronger your faith, the more confidently you will experience life, but also the greater the disruption should your belief be proved mistaken. That's why a belief based on truth is always best, and why you must remain open to reconsidering your faith as new information presents itself.

Faith helps you find peace in a world of competing points of view. It is a comforter that holds your hand as you walk through life. When emanating from a positive perspective founded primarily on reason and truth, faith is a force that helps propel that perspective into each successive day. Have faith!

18
Courage

"Immediately upon seeing her toddler fall off the pier, Lucy jumped into the dark, cold water, despite her inability to swim."

"Exhausted and unable to run any farther, the doe turned around, and with heavy, rapid breaths, defiantly confronted the ravenous wolf."

"Numb to the sights and sounds of his platoon's decimation, the battle-hardened Sergeant charged up the hill, his rifle spitting death."

Examples of courage? Most would say so. Courage is frequently defined by the act that takes place, as in "an act of courage." That's a misconception. Whether or not an act involves courage depends entirely on an individual's perspective, not on the event, itself.

"Even though Lucy has an exaggerated fear of drowning, she is determined to learn to swim. Fighting against her instincts, she releases her grip on the pool's Edge, and flails for all she's worth toward the opposite side."

"Despite the strong scent of danger, the nervous doe abandons the protective cover of dense scrub and cautiously enters the open meadow."

"His inner voice told him to run the other way, but he knew that if he did, the others would not have a chance. Many lives were spared, thanks to Sergeant Johnson's ultimate sacrifice."

These second examples demonstrate courage. They don't describe reflex actions, conditioned responses, or lesser of evils. They speak of choices that knowingly entail risk. True courage requires deliberation. True courage is the result of a decision-making process that examines the dangers, considers what needs to be done, and then proceeds despite fear. Someone without fear is not courageous, he is fearless. A courageous person is one who acts in the presence of fear, not in its absence.

Which do you think takes more courage, climbing to the top of a twelve-foot ladder or walking across a steel girder many stories above the ground? Doesn't it depend on who is doing what? A metal worker who frames skyscrapers each day of his life probably gives minimal thought to traversing a girder. He has little fear of it, therefore the act does not involve a courageous effort. Conversely, in order for me to install shutters on the second-story windows of my home, I have to summon all the courage I can muster, because I have a considerable fear of heights. Courage is subjective; it is relative to the individual and his or her interpretation of risk.

Courage is one of the finest attributes a person can have. Taking a personal risk and overcoming fear to help yourself or others show great character and strength of will. However, being courageous is not always a positive thing, especially when it's ill-conceived. The courage to commit suicide is certainly not productive, and electing to enter into a dangerous situation can reveal poor decision-making ability. The courage that is most admirable is courage that delivers a happy ending. More medals of honor are given to victors than to losers. This chapter is devoted to the type of courage that brings positive results.

To overcome a fear, you have two options:

1) You can alter your interpretation of the fear.
2) You can courageously proceed despite your fear.

Since fear is a personal definition, it can always be modified by thought. Some people can resolve a fear perception by simply dismissing it. Take young children, for example. Because they lack adult skills, they don't redefine their fears. Instead, they use auto suggestion, telling themselves things such as, *It won't hurt me* or *There's no such thing as...* or *I won't let it bother me*. Such rationalizations can effectively help an immature mind to overcome feared obstacles.

An adult is better equipped than a child. An adult has the intelligence to study a feared situation and come up with solid reasons for reducing apprehension. For example, the realization that it's statistically much safer to travel in an airplane than in a car can help counter the fear of flying, thereby lessening the courage that is required for a first-time flyer to board an airplane. When a positive truth replaces either an uncertainty or a negative imagination, fear can transform into a positive expectation. The cause of the fear does not have to change, nor does someone need to be courageous. Instead, the perception is revised. Whenever possible, this is the best method for defusing stress caused by fear.

Many fears are warranted, and real dangers should not have spins put on them to downplay their importance. Fear is a protective emotion that is beneficial when short-lived. Being fearful makes you cautious and keeps you from acting in ways that could worsen your situation. However, if you avoid every situation where there is risk, you will miss out on a lot of good living, and if you allow fear of some future possibility to disrupt your present state of mind, you will not enjoy life as you should. Rather than relying on creative definitions, sometimes you must call upon courage in order to acquire a more positive state of mind. Sometimes you have no choice but to rise above your fears and directly confront what lies before you.

If it sometimes feels like fear is overtaking you, it's almost always because you are looking with blinders, rather than seeing the entire picture. You must intercept such a perception. Fear that disrupts your state of being for an extended period of time is your enemy. Whenever the environment of your mind causes you to feel insecure, muster the courage to fight back, either by redefining the situation or by proceeding despite your fear. Fear is a negative weight that must be countered with positive action.

The time to quash a negative perception is the instant you become aware of it. If negatives are not intercepted early, you can easily become accustomed to feeling bad, acceding to that state of mind rather than doing something about it. Acceptance leads to tolerance, and bad feelings should never be tolerated; they should be fought with a vengeance. You have the power to refuse such feelings.

Each day you face an avalanche of contradictions and persuasions that weigh against your beliefs. It takes courage to march ahead in a world of confusion and calamity. Confronting the conflicts within your own mind also demands fortitude, because it is not easy to subdue powerful inner instincts. Negative thoughts are intimidating. When you are afraid, your negative perceptions are magnified, and the greater your fear, the more desperate your search for a safe hiding place. It takes very little to tip a positive attitude into negativism, and it takes a determined effort to tip it back. It's easy to rework your definitions when you're feeling tough, but when you are fearful, returning to a positive perspective takes more than logic; it takes courage.

When you are in a weakened state, your mind does whatever it can to keep this feeling from worsening. Your tendency is to set up a defense instead of making a counterattack. You think, I can't ignore this problem. I must worry about it. Things might not get better, so I have to prepare for the worst. When these are your thoughts, you have no chance at victory, and without relief, your stress will continue to build.

It takes courage to escape such a protective emotional state. Because fear is an instinctive response, the result of eons of human self-preservation, it's unnatural to do something to combat it. To override these strong impulses, you must confront your uncertainty. You must be willing to go in the opposite direction from where your protective emotions are taking you. The path of least resistance is to do nothing, and to allow your feelings to run their course, but if you want something better than what fate deals you, you will have to find the courage to rebuke those accustomed responses.

It would be great to be fearless in every situation, but you are truly a vulnerable creature and, regrettably, you will always be burdened with fear. When you need to be courageous, keep sight of your goals. Stand up to those things that could disrupt your Ultimate Perspective. Stay committed, and let that determination provide you with the strength to resist negativism, to face discouragement, and to take action.

19
Honor

The energy that you expend to maintain a positive state of mind must be regularly replenished, and to ensure that it's available every time you need it, you need a reliable source. What is yours? A positive attitude can be fueled by good music, breathtaking scenery, stimulating aromas, rich tastes, loving touches, and more. However, even though such stimuli are quite plentiful, they usually come to you only intermittently, rather than in a steady flow, and if your attitude relies solely on such external stimuli, then it is vulnerable, and at the mercy of forces over which you have no control.

In order to be sustained, it's best that a positive attitude be connected directly to a dependable resource. The world's limitless positive reserves can be tapped by looking for the positive subtleties in the moment, and then drawing upon them with a sustained appreciation, in the same way one savors a fine glass of wine, sip by sip.

Nevertheless, it would be better if you were not limited to external stimuli. If only your spark could be self-generated, not only would your happiness be less dependent on your appreciation skills, but you'd also have a resource that could be instantly accessed whenever needed. This can happen.

The most natural way to exude continual positive energy is by being happy with yourself. If you like yourself, your positive attitude is wired directly to a source of unlimited power: a healthy spirit. Therefore, it's essential that you work at attaining a positive self-image.

Self-esteem is self-respect. It's not self-adoration. Self-esteem is compatible with humility and a healthy ego. Regardless of the politically-correct brainwashing that society promulgates, a healthy and happy you is #1. The health of each "you" in the world determines the health of all. If you are unhappy with yourself, everyone has a problem.

A lot of good living is missed if you don't like yourself, if you can't enjoy your own company. You might not think it, but you are your best friend. You know yourself better than anyone else. You have the ability to read your own mind and to communicate with yourself. Who else has such intimate knowledge of your every like and dislike, your fears and stresses? Who else could put up with you every second, twenty-four/seven? But being your own best friend does not mean you are a good friend. A good friend would probably be more caring, understanding, and more accepting of the way you are. A good friend would provide you with encouragement whenever you need it. A good friend would be unfaltering, despite the mistakes you make. Are you a good friend to yourself, or have you placed too many conditions on that friendship?

Good friendships don't just happen, they are earned. For two friends to be loyal and supportive of one another, each must contribute sufficient positives to the other, so that the pluses in the relationship make the minuses inconsequential. One who has earned the honor of being someone else's good friend always deserves that honor.

You need to have sound reasons for liking yourself. Are your personal qualities the same as those you look for in others? Think about it. Take the time to introspect, and do so without putting yourself on trial (you wouldn't give yourself a fair one). Look at yourself without predetermining what you'll find, and try the best you can to make a neutral, honest evaluation.

You will likely zero in on the negative qualities that have been causing feelings of inferiority or guilt. Those are your handicaps. Most of them are not that serious, for they are nothing more than overcritical perceptions that can easily be altered through redefinitions. However, a few of your "faults," especially those causing guilt, have substance to back them up. Feelings of guilt might indicate the existence of negative truths about you, true imperfections that can't be redefined.

Guilt is a product of your conscience, which is your guardian of good behavior. Its purpose isn't to lower your self-esteem. Guilt is a ghost of the past whose purpose is to teach you and to guide your future behavior. It may feel like self-punishment, but it is not. It's a red flag that your conscience waves to let you know that you have performed contrarily to your internal moral code. It's a reminder that your thinking isn't aligned with your personal definitions. Substantive guilt is the result of not living up to the expectations you have of yourself.

All unresolved guilt is destructive, and eliminating it necessitates an earnest problem-solving approach. Your focus should not be on the guilt feeling; it should be on what has caused it. Guilt that arises from a breach of personal integrity diminishes your self-respect. When that happens, restoring a happy conscience requires that you acknowledge your mistake and change your behavior, rather than hiding behind creative definitions.

The best way to undo a substantive guilt feeling is to confront your errors honorably, and the best way to prevent guilt feelings is to be a person of honor. Honorable decision-making imparts self-respect, and honorable behavior projects your good qualities to the world. Being honorable is essential for liking yourself and for maintaining a continual spark of well-being.

Being honorable is not an endowment. You choose to be honorable. It isn't something that results from good genetics, nor does it relate to status, education, or wealth. Honor is a characteristic of noble personal values over which you exercise complete control. There is nothing more respected than honor. If you value it in others, you value it in yourself. If you despise others who act dishonorably, you despise your own dishonorable acts. Hence, it is not possible to deserve your own admiration unless you are truly honorable. To be honorable you must follow your conscience, perform as your soul says you should, acknowledge your weaknesses, correct your errors, and treat others as you would have them treat you.

Those who act contrary to their consciences dishonor themselves. They avoid introspection and deep contemplation because they know those thoughts will stir up feelings of guilt, feelings they prefer to keep under wraps. Such individuals have no choice but to function at the surface of their existence. Their quests for superficial gratifications result in reactionary behaviors, rather than behaviors that are well thought out. They seek rewards without giving sufficient thought to the ramifications of their acts. These unfortunates have little self-respect. Instead of pursuing happiness and subsequently finding it, a dishonorable person is limited to the pursuit. An all-encompassing happiness does not live on the surface; it lives deep within, in places where dishonorable people fear to look. Those whose consciences preclude deep thinking allow superficialities to lead them by their noses, which is why some end up with theirs high in the air.

The mark of an honorable person is integrity. Integrity is the result of doing the right thing, following the Golden Rule, and adopting the premise that one is rewarded in proportion to the service he provides. Those who choose to live in honor are respected by others, but more importantly, they glow within. The core of having a positive self-image is knowing that you are a person of honor.

By striving to be the person your conscience wants you to be, in both action and thought, that is who you become. You acquire a positive self-worth when you achieve self-respect, and you like yourself once you are likable. A good self-image is deserved when you are friendly, fair, kind, and you keep honor at the forefront.

If your soul is honorable, applaud that virtue and perceive yourself accordingly. If you don't have an honorable soul—even a small part of it—commit to becoming a better person, a person you can admire. Your greatest heroes and heroines gained their acclaim by being honorable. Had their successes been achieved through dishonesty, they could easily have been your villains. Because the choices you make determine the labels you wear, always think and act honorably.

20

Love

Imagine a ten-foot beam with a fulcrum in the middle— that's right, a teeter-totter—and picture one end weighted with negative feelings, the other with an equal weight of positives.

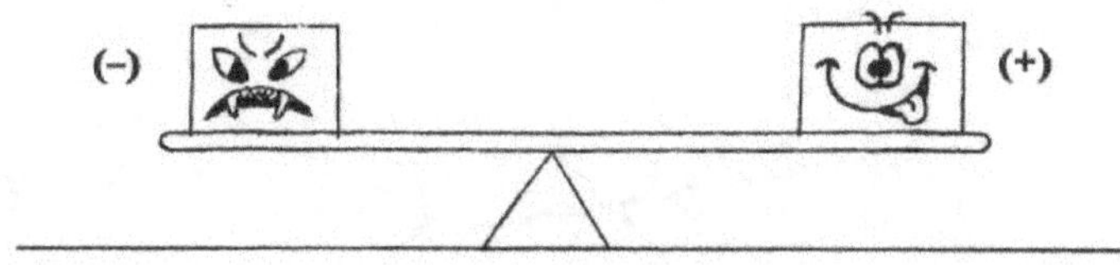

This image represents indifference, because the positive and negative feelings are in balance. If either end were to have weight added or subtracted, the beam would tilt, resulting in either a positive or a negative inclination. Since all balances are tenuous, a perfectly stable teeter-totter can only exist if something is done to secure the beam firmly in place, or if one end is so heavily weighted that it rests solidly on the ground.

Your feelings toward another individual depend on the inclination of such a beam: a variable, sentiment beam. If a perfectly level beam represents indifference, then being in love would be a sentiment that inclines the beam significantly toward the positive. Love has so many degrees of intensity that it's impossible to define the exact point where it materializes, so for now, let's just acknowledge that it exists as a range of positive sentiments.

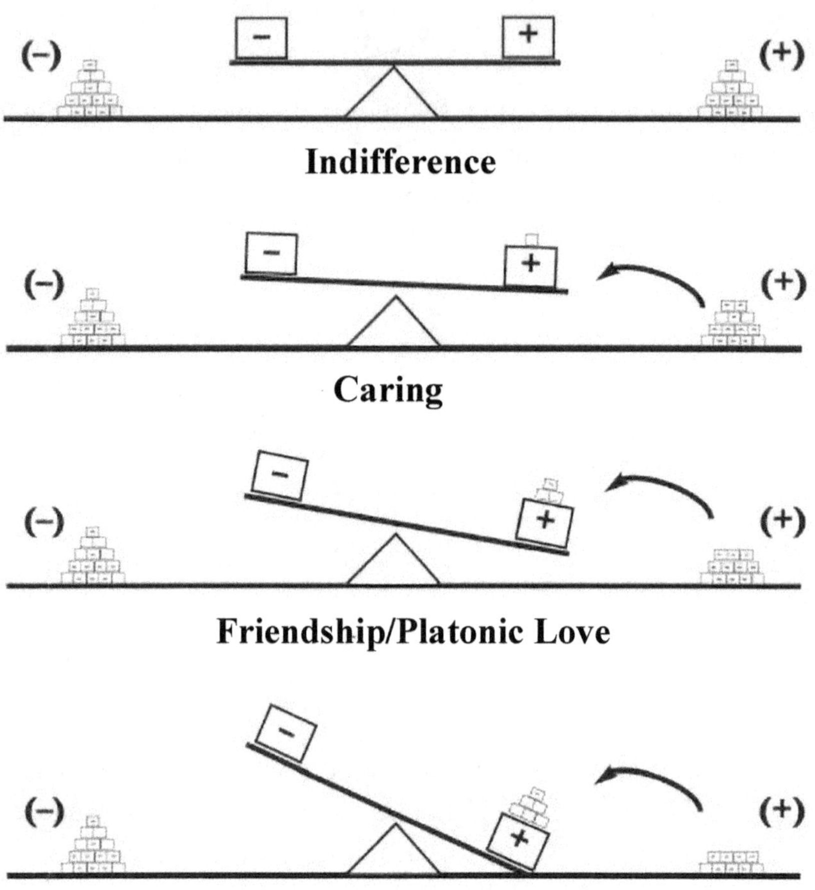

Adding weight to the plus side of a level sentiment beam will tip it slightly from neutral toward positive. Adding additional weight to that same side will increase the degree of tilt until the positive end eventually rests solidly on the ground. Throughout this range of tipping, varying degrees of affection result, from the type one might feel toward an appreciated friend, to a degree of love so overpowering that the love is unconditional.

When love is heavily weighted with positive feelings, any counteracting negatives have little or no influence. No matter what the weight of those negatives, as long as the positives weigh significantly more, good feelings will dominate and satisfy a heart's need. This is simple logic. All you have to do to be happily in love is acquire a positive tilt and then maintain it by keeping that end of your sentiment beam loaded with positive weight.

If only it could be that easy. Maintaining a lasting, romantic love is not a simple matter, because the love emotion is not logical, and other priorities gain importance as a couple becomes comfortable in their relationship. What at first might seem to be an invincible love will, over time, undergo a waning that results in a tipping back toward neutrality. This is the doom of many a great romance.

The heaviest child on a teeter-totter has the ability to hold his playmate helplessly in the air while he smugly keeps his end on the ground. Initially, such an imbalance can be fun for both playmates, but the enjoyment is always short-lived. There is more sustained excitement to be had when both children take turns rising into the air, and then returning back to the ground. Similarly, a love that has its periodic ups and downs is more stimulating than one that is stationary.

There are shortcomings in every relationship, but shortcomings are not always harmful. A lasting love feeds hungrily on the interplay of both positives and negatives. In this chapter you will learn how a minor see-sawing of the sentiment beam is good, because it keeps love on its toes and, most importantly, it stimulates a couple's appreciation for one another.

Love is tenuous. Take away some positives and/or add a few negatives and the intensity will diminish. For all lovers, even during the best of times, negatives ominously loom at the opposite end of the sentiment beam. When a relationship is strong, those negatives are inconsequential, but should the weight of positives lighten, the negatives will gain significance. Even a minor tilt toward the negative can be disruptive.

Ah, the tingling elation. Alas, the gut-wrenching pain! Love encompasses every extreme. While most people covet love, it's also understandable why some will do anything to avoid it. Love is a gamble. Love has the power to independently create or destroy a person's happiness. It's responsible for murders and suicides, it can destabilize a primary perspective, and it's nearly impossible to control once it has taken over. The quest for love is like a lottery, where winners win big but the odds of winning are not very good. You'd think no one would play a game that has such a low probability for success, yet people do, and will continue to do, despite their losses.

The best odds for winning at love exist when each partner needs something that the other partner can provide, and when the satisfying of those needs creates mutual appreciation. Now some people consider dependency on another person as portraying weakness. That may be so. Although it's been said, "Love isn't for the faint-hearted," it seems the least secure individuals are the ones most attracted to it. Someone who is insecure certainly has the most to gain from what a dependable love can provide.

Conversely, there are those who cherish their independence, and don't want feelings dictating what they do. Some see strong emotions as drawbacks to self-determination—in other words, as barriers to personal freedom.

If you are among those who choose to curb their emotions, then you are the type of person who would prefer to have your sentiment beam locked in place, so that it can't tilt one way or the other, thus ensuring consistent, uncomplicated feelings toward other people. If that's what you've been trying to do, you've learned that many positives and negatives are not within your control, and your locking mechanism has had to be constructed out of a firm resolve to not allow your emotions to run amok.

When taking into consideration the poor odds of stumbling into an idyllic relationship, and the likelihood that falling in love will be accompanied by a significant amount of grief, achieving neutral feelings might be the wisest goal to set. In any situation, the greater the heights reached, the greater the potential fall. When you are in love you are vulnerable. As a love intensifies, the risk of being hurt increases. A loving relationship can't be taken for granted, because losing at love is so painful. But the lure of love—so tempting! There's no question that having success at it is like winning the lottery. In order to live your life to the max, risks have to be taken, so let's see what can be done to tip the odds in your favor.

Sexual attraction is the most common impetus that steers one toward a potential mate. It opens the door to that more heartfelt feeling, love. Because physical interest accompanies romantic love, it is sometimes hard to distinguish which is playing the dominant role, especially in the early stages of a relationship. But for the purposes of this chapter, sexual desire will be considered a subordinate component of that more enduring prize, spiritual love.

What is it that accounts for extreme love feelings? The answer may not be what you would expect. You are wrong if you believe it is an abundance of positives in a relationship. Actually, the most intense love feelings are the result of negatives. That's right, negatives. How can negatives be responsible for making you feel so good? The answer lies within the concept of cravings.

For example, being parted from a loved one can bring considerable heartache. When lovers reunite after having longed for one another, the reunion always results in strong, positive feelings. However, as those emotions run their course, the intensity of those feelings lessens. Unmet needs and desires are what cause cravings, therefore, the key to maintaining an intense love is the perpetuation of need and desire. Without need and desire, a heartfelt love will eventually tip toward indifference, and the erasure of need and desire is the surest way to destroy an active love. It's the maintenance of love cravings that keeps love dynamic. Love is strongest when an element of heartache or yearning persists.

New love is always exhilarating because there's so much to stimulate both the mind and the senses. A new, shared love initiates the satisfying of one's love needs, and the sexual component adds excitement and further gratification. But even with all these positives coming about, negatives persist in the form of needs that have not yet been met, and also the feelings of uncertainty that are inherent in a new relationship. These negatives are insecurities that tease the emotions, helping them seesaw up and down, thereby creating disturbances that, even though unsettling, feed continual interest into the relationship.

As a relationship matures, cravings become satisfied. Surety replaces uncertainty, which results in a leveling of emotions. This stabilization translates into a waning of excitement. As long as lovers have reasons to be appreciative of one another, a love will continue to grow, but once a relationship feels safe, there's a tendency for appreciations to lessen and for complacency to set in.

Love is an itch. It feels so good to have an itch scratched, but as the itch is satisfied, the pleasure of the scratching diminishes.

Love is skydiving, bungee jumping, and "streaking." It's not only the act itself that's stimulating; it's also the excitement of putting yourself at risk, and then the reward that results from successfully accomplishing the feat.

Love is an intense appreciation and dependency. It can't exist without need and desire, therefore it requires negative counter-forces to keep it going and growing.

Every good feeling has a negative element behind it. For example, the enjoyment of eating is linked to the discomfort of being hungry. I am reminded of this fact every time I eat at a Don Shula's Steakhouse. Whenever I go to one, I make sure I'm famished beforehand, because I can't resist partaking in the Porterhouse Challenge: 48 ounces of mouth-watering lusciousness! As soon as the juicy cut is set in front of me, I voraciously dig in, but as the minutes pass by, the intensity of my appreciation steadily lessens, even though the flavor remains consistent throughout the meal. As my appetite becomes satiated, my desire for steak decreases until I eventually reach the point where I can't eat another bite. Dessert? Fuhgeddaboudit! In fact, by the time I push away from the table, Porterhouse is no longer on my list of appreciations. This happens every time! Amusingly, any vow of reformation that I make to the cholesterol gods is short lived and replaced in time by renewed cravings for another Shula's session. The return of my hunger (a negative) brings a return of my appreciation (a positive).

There are some people who can sustain a high dining appreciation throughout even a huge meal. A while back I watched a television documentary about a gourmet dining club whose members would feast for hours on fine foods and wines, purging themselves as needed so they could dine all evening without becoming full. Unlike with bulimics, these people didn't kneel in front of toilets to keep their weight down. Their motivation was to prolong the pleasure of dining. They were serious about these events and knew that becoming full would end their ability to enjoy the many delicacies offered to them. To fully appreciate their feasts, they had to delay becoming satiated. Similarly, a person who can sustain a need to love and be loved has a hunger that resists satiation. For love to endure, need must endure.

The sentiment beam illustrations demonstrate how love intensity varies according to the weight of perceived positives in a relationship. However, the inclination also depends on the weight of negatives on the beam's opposite end. The degree of love that you feel is determined by external influences, by the positives and negatives that you define, and by your perspective. If any of these factors reduces the amount of positive weight, or adds to the negative weight, the beam will tilt toward the negative side, creating anxious feelings.

Actually, negatives are love's greatest supporters, because when insecure feelings arise, the instinctive place to gain security is in the protective arms of someone who cares about you, and also because negatives have the power to awaken love feelings that have become dormant. When negatives threaten you, they rejuvenate appreciation for everything that's at risk and for everything that has been good. When your security is jeopardized, your feelings naturally intensify.

No matter what's responsible for a negative tipping of the sentiment beam, it's a return to positive that keeps a love from dying. It's a return to positive that can make love even stronger than before. A love that's allowed to fatigue for any reason withers. A love that rebounds from a step back has the opportunity to move two steps forward.

Love is most appreciated when it doesn't come easily, but that doesn't mean that in order to have strong, loving feelings you should welcome negatives into your relationship. Negative tugs awaken you from complacency, but that's where their benefit ends. Never intentionally introduce negatives into a relationship in order to make it stronger, even though negatives have participated in the creation of your most cherished feelings. Just realize that in order to perpetuate those feelings, it's necessary to find ways to maintain your longings and appreciation.

Cupid understands how love works. He knows that a bow must be drawn before an arrow can fly to its target. He knows that someone must be struck with his arrow before love can be felt. Unless there's a yearning, there can be no satisfaction; without first experiencing insecurity, it's not possible to feel secure; without an arrow first plucking the heartstrings, love can't resonate into a beautiful song.

In order to have a lasting, intense love—a continued, new love feeling—both partners must have sustained cravings, and both must be willing to scratch each other's "itches." Here are conditions that promote such a love:

1) The presence of emotional hunger
2) The ability to willingly give
3) The ability to graciously receive
4) Appreciation for one's partner
5) Respect for one's partner
6) A willingness to face and resolve problems as a team
7) A willingness to share thoughts and feelings
8) The perception of compatibility
9) The ability to adapt and be flexible
10) The ability to entertain one's partner
11) The ability to entertain oneself

What order of priority would you give these conditions? Would you add to or subtract from this list? Would your loved one's priorities be similar to yours?

The conditions in this list relate to both love intensity and durability. They are, of course, conditions from the author's perspective, not from yours or anyone else's. Someone who is more private with his or her feelings would certainly have a much different list than one who chooses to openly express their emotions. For some, love is totally a feeling, whereas for others it's primarily an intellectualization. The significance of all of this: If one partner's list doesn't resemble the other's list, both will be frustrated.

Opposites attract, but they make a poor natural match. Large differences in personalities and perspectives might make for a stimulating relationship, and opposite strengths and weaknesses do have the positive effect of evening out each other's shortcomings, but the joining of opposites also makes conflict inevitable. The more dissimilar a couple's needs, the more unlikely their individual needs will be met. The closer two people are in their reasoning and in their goals, the more empathy and understanding between them. Two becoming one is most assured when partners have psychological make-ups that readily meld.

Anything short of a complete, dual fulfillment will leave at least one partner shy of their happiness goal. However, as long as both lovers have their most important criteria met, a relationship of opposites can be positively weighted. A few strong pluses can override a number of lesser negatives, but the further away from having a comfortable compatibility, the closer a couple is to conflict. If your number-one criterion is intimacy but your partner can't express intimacy, the relationship will never seem adequate to you. On the other hand, although you would, thereby, be unfulfilled, your partner might be completely happy with things the way they are. You could be your partner's ideal person, while your partner is inadequate for you, and vice versa.

Theoretically, a satisfying love is easy to achieve. All someone has to do is find a compatible mate and then work with that person to augment the positives they naturally share. Unfortunately, such a match rarely happens. New love is a nearsighted affliction, and the vast majority of facts that two people discover about each other come to light some distance down the road, usually after marriage vows have been exchanged. However, if both partners can be dedicated to satisfying each other's most important needs, and to nurturing tolerance, patience, and appreciation, then any relationship can be intensely satisfying.

A perfect love doesn't require a perfect compatibility. The presence of occasional conflict doesn't mean that consistent, gratifying feelings are not attainable. Any concept of "perfection," when applied to such imperfections as human beings, is an illusion anyway. Perfection is an individual interpretation. One person's "perfect spaghetti sauce" is "too much oregano" for another. Because love is a matter of personal definition and perspective, one has the ability to perceive an imperfect match as one that fits quite perfectly.

A love relationship requires the reciprocation of love. You can love someone who does not love you, but it's impossible to love another and not desire to be loved in return. So, for a couple to have love fulfillment, it necessitates each partner being able to give and take. The happiest couples feed positively off one another. They are the solution to each other's problems. A relationship grows stronger when lovers help each other out.

In instances where basic personality types are dissimilar, the support that one partner naturally provides may not be what is needed by the other partner, but that doesn't mean the couple does not have the capability of being a satisfying match. With caring and respect, two dissimilar people can learn to satisfy each other. In the presence of a mutual love, neither one should have a problem making an effort to please the other, even if those actions are not instinctive. Communicating needs and then having them taken care of is how opposites become compatible. What is specifically given or received does not have to be the same for each one, and every thirst does not have to be quenched. All that is important is that both parties have their most essential needs met.

Love abounds when partners willingly make sacrifices in order to foster an exchange of appreciation. These acts should not be seen as sacrifices, however. To insure that sharing continues to cycle, the perception of "sacrifices" in these instances must be redefined as "gifts." Also, it is important to focus more on what you can give, rather than what you will receive. You only have control over the giving part of an exchange. By giving to someone you care about, you make a direct, positive impact on that person's perception of you, which then encourages that person to provide a kindness in return.

Continual negativity destroys a relationship. Negativity is tolerable only when there are compensating, positive breaks. In a lengthy tug-of-war contest, a smart team allows its members to take turns, briefly pausing to re-brace their feet, improve their grip on the rope, or take quick recuperating breaths. When this is done properly, the overall team effort remains strong and steady, even though no single member makes a constant pull. A team that doesn't allow such pauses may make a more uniform effort, but they tire more quickly, making them ultimately less effective than the team whose members are allowed to make small, strategic adjustments. Similarly, a love that fights continually against negatives, without a chance to recoup positive energy, inevitably wears out. There has to be some break in the negativity and some exchange of affection and appreciation in order for a relationship to endure.

Almost as great a detriment to a relationship as a persistent, negative assault is a love that maxes-out. A love that runs out of steam eventually drifts back toward neutrality, or even negativity. When this happens, the cause of the weakening isn't as obvious as when there's a blatant reason for a decline in affection. Love can fade away, leaving a couple clueless as to how it happened. A love can be defeated by a steady pull of obvious negatives, but it can also die from a not-so-obvious lessening of positives.

The joining of psychological twins may make for the most compatible initial relationship, but the more similar two people are, the greater the odds that their relationship will eventually become routine. However, a waning of love intensity does not happen only to lovers who lack contrast. Eventual loss of love is the bane of all matchups. This fading is usually the result of predictability and lack of challenge, or, in other words, lack of change. Change brings vitality to the moment, and change makes it easier to put aside thoughts that are self-defeating. A relationship that remains interesting keeps pushing forward. If a couple can remain appreciative and experience new adventures and new scenery together, their love should intensify over time.

A perfect love relationship is not as implausible as it may seem. For one thing, most lovers, even opposites, do have a significant compatibility or they would not have fallen in love in the first place. For another, even though humans are incredibly diverse in their mode of expression, common elements become evident as the layers of their individuality peel away. Although those inner layers may be difficult to access, somewhere beneath everyone's crust is a soul that belongs to the same brotherhood. That dimension is where empathy overrides ego, and seemingly diverse perspectives become like-minded. That is where love can achieve perfection.

Is it possible for two unique souls to reach that dimension together? Yes, but not by chipping away at each other's complicated structure. That level is reached by rejecting chaotic stimuli and attaining perceptions that are pure and simple. It is reached by seriously entering the moment. Casting off cloaks of bias and desire exposes a person's pure being. When two souls are thus bared, it's easier for them to relate to each other and to express their feelings. Entering the realm of "now" prioritizes the moment and allows a couple to focus on the purest of concerns. This is the best way to awaken consciousness and to connect hearts.

There is never a shortage of things to appreciate, once individuals tune-in to the harsh realities of life and the extreme importance of now.

When the moment is given top priority, one cannot help but be appreciative. When two hearts share the moment, and thus join in common thought, true empathy is born, and disconnected desires can then integrate.

It is impossible to be blessed with a deep love and not feel threatened by anything that would interfere with it. Even during the best of times, underlying fears and uncertainties cause negative tugs. The stresses that those tugs create raise a couple's appreciation for one another by stimulating thoughts, such as:

I'd be nothing without him.

or

I don't know how we'll get through this.

or

I can't stand the thought of losing her.

Appreciation is the glue for maintaining a love bond. The more one lover appreciates the other, the more profound the love feelings. As long as the maintenance of love is given the same effort as the initial achievement, it will remain inspired. A partner who is appreciative gives love willingly and receives it graciously. When you appreciate your partner, you see perfections rather than imperfections. Appreciation overrides negatives, reduces criticism, and increases well-being. It washes stress from a relationship and inspires affection.

Both logic and emotion contribute to a love framework. There are many variables to contend with. But if two people can agree on nothing more than the importance of maintaining a healthy, lifelong relationship, and if they remain appreciative of the contributions each makes to the other, then their love experience will be rewarding, moment to moment, regardless of each individual's concept of love.

When one feels love and gratitude for a partner, it should not be difficult to step slightly out of one's comfort zone to demonstrate those feelings, especially when there is a return of gratitude. But what if there's no reciprocation? A relationship becomes threatened when one partner feels unappreciated and thereby loses the perception of balance.

Whenever a relationship is unbalanced, the adversely affected partner can overcome it by altering his personal definitions, by striving for greater tolerance and patience, and by adapting personal needs to better match the needs of the partner. Too often one partner tries to improve the situation by attempting to change the habits or psychological makeup of the other. That will not work. You can't expect that your partner will adapt to you; you only have control over what you think and do.

The fulfillment of your every emotional need shouldn't be the responsibility of your partner. Rather than allowing yourself to be disappointed with your partner, especially if there are many things in the relationship for which to be grateful, there are times when it's your own perspective that needs adjustment. Every individual has imperfections, yet, under the right circumstances, any partner can be perceived by the other as being quite ideal. The majority of failed relationships are the fault of inflexible, negative definitions, rather than one partner's failure to make a positive contribution.

In summary, life's too precious to be spent in a mediocre situation. Any valuable relationship that tilts negatively should not be tolerated for an instant. You must be committed to doing whatever can be done to enrich your moments, and to discover positives that will compensate for life's tragedies. When things begin to tilt negatively, find a way to reverse the trend, and don't be frustrated if every craving isn't satisfied. Remain stimulated. If you feel frustrated, take action by turning to the moment. Allow your needs and desires to surface so that you can identify them specifically. Quiet them by molding your perspective in a way that helps you satisfy them. If a rewarding love is your quest, then work at being appreciative and also at being a sincere giver of love. Communicate your needs to your partner, and work at building a loving relationship wherein both of you can have your most important needs met. You can't help each other if you don't know what those needs are and how important they are. Do all you can to redefine the negatives you perceive in your partner, and together make plans that will keep your relationship interesting.

21

Contentment

Upon achieving their goals, many find themselves still unfulfilled. That's because their accomplishments don't alter the underlying reality, and for them, reality isn't something to celebrate. Such an inability to achieve satisfaction is sad. At some point, a person needs to believe, "I'm content."

Now for the most difficult part of your changeover: **YOU MUST BE CONTENT WITH REALITY!**

Whether it's by accepting things as they are, or by making constructive, personal definitions to improve your interpretations, this is how it must be. Reality is the moment, and moments are all you have, therefore you must respect reality, whatever it is.

What is reality? Plain and simple, it is truth. Reality is the prime absolute. However, because a mind cannot experience reality without making a biased interpretation of it, reality is always distorted to some degree. Once the mind gets involved, reality becomes a conjecture rather than an absolute.

It's nearly impossible to be one-hundred-percent objective about anything pertaining to yourself. Your interpretations are as you choose to make them. Your perspective is the world according to you. You define which TV programs are entertaining, which books are interesting, and which activities are enjoyable. You experience reality, but it is a reality that has been personalized. Your wish is to have that reality come as close as possible to an imagined ideal. This is good. As a matter of fact, it's what this book is all about. But this noble intent can go awry if taken too far. Reality must be accepted in order for your perspective to be stable.

Through your definitions you have the power to manipulate reality to some degree—primarily through your immediate realm of influence: the space between your ears. But there is a lot of reality out there, and it has a mind of its own. Events beyond your control can make it difficult to maintain a positive expectation, and even an Ultimate Perspective cannot smooth every roughness. Sometimes you have no option but to limit the depth of your thinking, or to avoid some thoughts altogether, because dwelling on harsh truths can elicit emotions that are more than what a positive perspective can handle. Sometimes you just need to tell yourself, "It is what it is."

In order to protect your positive energy, you have no other option but to accept the negatives that can't be changed. There is no process for doing this; it has to be an outright choice. There is a limit to what you can control, and sometimes you just have to go with the flow, wherever that happens to take you. Everything will not go your way, and you will fall short of many goals. You have the option to fight losing causes, and watch your positive energy disappear, or you can accept those no-win situations and preserve your positive energy.

Contentment is your goal. It's an elusive one if you allow it to be, but it can also be realized immediately, if that's what you want. It's one of the few goals that can be attained simply by flipping a switch in your head. You are in charge of your expectations.

Whether they are regarding personal accomplishments, feathering your nest, or fighting your foes, you determine when the job is finished or when you've done enough. The only criteria are your own. It is simply a decision of how you choose to think and feel.

Regardless of the pluses or minuses that befall you, reality is in charge. You can fight it and be miserable, or you can work with it and be at peace. You can perceive reality as standing in the way of your happiness, or you can see it as the environment in which you will do the best you can. It's up to you at what point in your endeavors you will finally say to yourself, "I'm content."

22
Tidbits

Dirty Words:

Whenever you start a thought process with *What if...,* you are looking for trouble. These words begin a conjecture that creates stress that otherwise wouldn't exist. You already have way too much stress; why create even more for yourself? That's what happens when your mind goes out of its way to find reasons to be anxious or fearful. Avoid thoughts of *What if...*

Even more self-defeating are *Woulda, Coulda,* and *Shoulda.* Delete these obscene words from your vocabulary! You perpetuate negative feelings when you relive disappointments and wish things had turned out differently. Move on. Don't use these dirty words!

Easing A Crisis:

Accentuating the positives in your life is the quickest and most predictable way to ease the stress of a crisis. When you are in a crisis, you have a frame of mind that hungers for positive feelings. This humble state is extra-receptive to any positive force. Focusing on your blessings will immediately improve how you feel and how you are able to cope. You'll not rid yourself of your crisis by embracing positive thoughts, but by switching your vision to the positives in your life, you'll certainly lessen the negative impact that your crisis would otherwise make on you.

Regarding Depression:

A state of depression is more difficult to deal with than a Crisis, because a depressed person does not visualize positives. With depression, negatives take over the mind and push positives away, resulting in the depression perpetuating itself. Even a minor state of depression is dangerous, because it can become more severe as negative thoughts upstage everything that has the potential to create a better mindset.

When you are melancholic, you are less receptive to good news. You can know that there are positives in the world, yet not have the desire to embrace them. A disheartened frame of mind can even interpret good news as yet another negative.

To break free from the depression doldrums, you must first experience a single, positive feeling upon which momentum can build. Begin by taking a look at your primary perspective to see what has changed or where you have slipped. Revisit your appreciations. Make adjustments that will initiate a more positive mental state. If you cannot rework your thoughts on your own, seek out a close friend, a professional counselor, or a doctor who will prescribe a medication that will either dull your anxiety or lift your attitude to a sufficient degree that you become more receptive to the layering of positive thoughts. The important thing is that you find that initial spark, whatever it may be, so you can then build upon it.

Lateral Thinking:

Lateral thinking is a problem-solving option for the times when answers can't be found through a customary, straightforward approach. Patterned thinking can guide you from point A directly to point B, but a crow's flight is not the only route that will get you where you want to go. Lateral thinking is non-direct. It is looking at your problem from an alternate angle. It is taking a few steps to the side to get a better view of what you're trying to see.

Lateral thinking involves examining peripheral facts that you have not yet considered. It includes asking other people for their less-biased opinions, so that you then have new ideas to contemplate. Lateral thinking constitutes erasing your notepad and starting over with fresh, imaginative alternatives. It is separating yourself from the emotional constraints and prejudices that have been chaining you to an ineffective train of thought.

Using a lateral point of view is looking at a situation as though you were some distance away, similar to being a football coach sitting in a box seat high above the playing field. From this elevated vantage point, a coach sees things differently than those who are down on the turf. Not only does he view the game from a broader perspective, but he is also removed from the sideline circus.

Whenever you have difficulty coming up with a solution to a problem, think laterally for a few minutes. Imagine yourself as an observer of what is taking place, rather than as being involved. Abandon everything that you have been thinking, and try to come up with entirely new thoughts. Lateral thinking distances you from the emotions that block your creativity, and it helps to end the rehashing of dead-end options so that you can then start over with fresh ideas.

Fighting Your Ego:

Sometimes it's your ego that holds you back. Your ego can defeat you in many ways, the most common being when it refuses to admit that you are the one responsible for what you are feeling. In order to improve your state of mind, you have to acknowledge that you have the ability to be stronger than you've been, which is a humbling admission that you've allowed yourself to become weak in the first place. When you are already bruised, that realization is one more kick in the ego ribs, but you need to make that admission if you want things to get better. Don't let your ego keep you from achieving greater happiness. Wage war against your ego.

Write It Down:

I'm a firm believer in the power of the pen—your pen. Putting thoughts on paper is a great aid to lateral thinking. It's also an effective way to outwit your ego. By the time your thoughts travel from your brain, through your arm, and out your fingertips, poisonous thinking becomes somewhat filtered, and the words that emerge onto paper are more representative of what you truly think.

If you are angry or despondent, some of your first words may express erratic thoughts, because a whirlwind mind moves faster than the tip of one's pen, but as your mind slows down to match the speed of what you are writing, the script will get better and better. Whenever you are at a mental impasse, just start writing, even if you don't know where it will lead. You'll be surprised what is revealed. Take out a pad of paper and see if this isn't true.

Meaningful Work:

The day-to-day prevention of negative thoughts is most readily accomplished by doing meaningful work. The positive feelings that come from performing a task that's meaningful last well beyond the time spent on the task. Oppositely, if you don't enjoy the work that you do, the energy spent fighting those negative perceptions will wear on you all day and beyond. Your mind needs to be busy and occupied by positive forces. If you don't have meaningful work to do, strive to attain it, and keep in mind the fact that most negativity is the result of personal definitions that can be improved.

The Flip Side:

Just as you have the ability to apply only those definitions that will reinforce your perspective, an author has the ability to present only those facts that will support his claims. Keep in mind that there is a flip side to nearly every example used in The Changeover.

For instance, the negative effect of collectives has been emphasized in this book, and that is because group doctrines tend to interfere with personal enlightenment, yet there are many ways in which collectives benefit their individual members. When people unite to support one another, or to achieve a common goal, then that aspect of a group is a very positive force that can augment a primary perspective.

If reading this book has created any negative image that didn't exist beforehand, please undo it now. You interpreted it as being a negative only because I didn't reveal its flip side. My purpose has been to get my points across, not to add to your negative perceptions. Remember, for every negative there is also a counteracting positive, a Yin for every Yang.

Wrap Up: Better Moments

You can't control all situations, but you can control how you respond to them. Whenever you feel stressed, escape that emotional state by switching to a less personal "World" perspective. Look at your situation critically, but not negatively. Set your feelings aside when evaluating your circumstances so that you can make better decisions. Accept the fact that negatives do exist, and keep in mind that it's up to you how they are handled. Uphold truth, not falsehood. Acknowledge the good that surrounds you when it becomes evident. Acknowledge the negatives also, but strive to find sufficient positives to make those negatives a lesser part of your total perceptions.

Throughout *The Changeover* you have been challenged to rethink your opinions and your endeavors. You have read that personal definitions are not sacred and that you should reevaluate yours to see if changes are in order. The suggestions that have been offered have not been meant to mold you into an unrealistic ideal or an endorser of the author's prejudices, but rather to free you from old habits that have been limiting your potential. Your unique interpretations and needs are the determining factors for your life perspective. Hopefully, you are reconstructing that perspective so that it will work better for you.

It is what you choose to think, not what the world forces upon you, that is responsible for how you feel. Thoughts produce both sweet and bitter fruit. You have the power to either create or destroy your happiness, for you are the master of those thoughts. You now must decide how you will use your new knowledge and what you will change.

There are no words powerful enough to rework a lifetime of mental programming in one fell swoop. This book's ending is only your beginning. If you have made a commitment to build a more positive primary perspective, that is not the same as having achieved one. Your inspiration must be converted into actualization. I suggest that you go through this book once again, but this time with your mind in a "study" mode, rather than a "reading" mode. Spend time contemplating each realization, so that it becomes more firmly imprinted in your mind.

Don't just determine what you need to do; make those changes and, from then on, live them.

You might choose to use your positive energy and heightened appreciation to generate new accomplishments and prosperity. Then again, maybe what you would rather do is dump your stress and take off on a new path. If you are unsure about what you want to change, just begin capturing a few rainbows, and then let those successes teach you more about yourself. Whatever you do, it's time to permanently lighten your mental load so that you can free your potential.

Allow yourself to begin anew. Allow yourself to become healthier. A good life is attracted to good thoughts. It's against your best interests to think negatively or to limit yourself to microscopic details. Instead, ride the currents high above the hills and valleys, so that you can view the totality of life's offerings.

How do you know if you are on course? By periodically evaluating how you feel and determining if that feeling is good enough for you. Are you working on your goals, or are they working you? Are you stressing too much? Are you playing too little? Are you applying yourself, or do you lack motivation? In a nut shell, if you are unhappy, you are not making the right choices and you need to change direction.

Humans are the most adaptable of all Earth's creatures. What we can't handle by way of technology, we handle by determination. However, our seeming ability to survive everything that is thrown at us makes us somewhat complacent. There are times when we acclimate ourselves to situations that should not be tolerated. It's easy to adapt, easy to become lulled and to lose inspiration. Everywhere around us are examples of people who endure much more than they should, just because they have become accustomed to their plight. Has this happened to you? Consider your own situation and make sure you haven't also adapted to a negative conformity.

Take a good look at where you are, what you have accomplished, and where you seem to be going. If you are not content with the reality you see, find something that you can change—any single thing that you can either alter or redefine—and then act on it. Step back, w-a-a-a-y back, and look at the bigger picture. You don't have to resolve your problems in order to begin lessening their impact on your life. Solutions will present themselves as you broaden your perspective and gain inspiration.

All you need is a tiny spark to ignite you. The specific story that unfolds isn't that important, so long as it's an improved story, a better reality.

Your reality experience is a filtered awareness of what life's all about. Your reality is what you see (perception), what you feel (interpretation), and what you have become (perspective). There's nothing else. It's really very simple; It's all within you. You are the one making it so complicated. Reconsider the world, the moment, and your mortality, and do whatever it takes to make this moment, the next moment, and all your remaining moments the experiences they rightly should be.

Moments can always be made more meaningful. In fact, they can become one-hundred-percent meaningful if you choose to make them so. Stop setting yourself up for *I shoulda…woulda…, coulda….* With a little determination you can craft an improved perspective, a better reality.

As soon as you make the decision to feel better, you will experience:

1) A heightened awareness
2) An unveiling of positives
3) Greater appreciation for things once taken for granted
4) Improvements to your personal definitions
5) A more realistic and accepting self-image
6) A better today and a more promising tomorrow

Achieving a positive primary perspective is absolutely the best thing you will ever do for yourself, but after you have created one, there will likely be a time when it will no longer have your full attention, and you'll cease putting effort into its maintenance. Your positive energy will then fade, because negatives will continue to appear, and, as you know, negatives are more influential than positives. They will chip away at your positive outlook without your being aware of what's happening. At some point you will realize, *I'm in a negative state again.*

Being in a funk is always the result of a failure to maintain one's positive definitions and one's appreciations. When you catch yourself in that mindset, you will once again have to purge your negativism by revisiting your database to make definition changes that will return you to a better state of mind. After you have made those corrections, search your soul for anything that may be lacking, and fill any voids with the appreciations that are simple, cheap, and plentiful.

The world is a chaotic place, and it harbors many adverse elements that work against you. To have the life you would like to have, you must adjust to those annoyances by rhythmically gathering positives, one by one, so that you continue to collect as many as you can and, therefore, receive the greatest possible reward. It's not always easy to be appreciative, but that's what you must remind yourself to be. Being appreciative is the prerequisite for contentment.

It takes time for a new outlook to become second nature, and you don't want to return to your habitual ways. Periodically review this book to remind yourself of the positive and negative forces that affect you. Write your strongest needs down and place them on your desk. Frame the word "PERSPECTIVE" and hang it where you will see it first thing in the morning and last thing at night. Do whatever it takes to remain focused.

Beware of negative thinking, because negativism breeds negativism. When you become overly critical, you find more things to criticize. Subconsciously, the mind seeks to confirm its programming. This search for confirmation can easily result in the creation of negative definitions that will crowd out positive ones, making it harder to be optimistic, harder to be happy. That's the exact opposite of what you need.

Negatives are real, and they will surely bring you down if you allow them to pile on top of one another. Whenever you become aware of a negative thought, don't leave it untouched or the next negative will add to it, progressing into a downward spiral. Instead, when experiencing a negative, even a minor one, immediately temper it, or compensate for it by adding at least one positive counter-perception, so that a negatively-weighted perspective does not result. No negative thought is trivial. In fact, the innocuous negatives are the most dangerous because they are so plentiful.

Although your inner voice knows what you must do, there are times when you can't hear it, and an outside stimulus is needed to amp up that logic. Don't be afraid to discuss your problems and fears with others who have the skill to reinforce a positive outlook, and avoid those who would cry with you. You need encouragement, not sympathy. Seek out those who project a healthy, positive mindset. Seek out those who have faith in their beliefs, and turn to these people whenever you feel discouraged. Use their positive energies to point you in a better direction.

You've been given a lot to think about, but it all comes down to one simple theme that's been interspersed throughout this presentation, and that is the importance of building an honest, positive outlook on life, so that your moments are the best they can be. I hope this message helps you achieve greater happiness. I could have added other chapters to this book, such as Friendship, Contemplation, Religion, Motivation, Relaxation, Recovery, Wealth, Liberty, and more, but I have left them for you to write.

It's now time to become the person you want to be, so that you are a healthier, happier, true individual. It's time to begin a life of discovery, and it's time to make your mind a prism that splits ordinary light into all colors of the spectrum. It's time for better moments.

Begin with a new canvas. Paint your perspective the way you would like it to look. Create an image that will inspire you for the rest of your life. Paint toughness, desire, love, energy, truth, honor, appreciation, tolerance, acceptance, contentment, and, above all, paint rainbows. Build your own Ultimate Perspective, and then be steadfast in making it durable. Undergo a changeover and live the POSSIBLE dream.

NOT THE END!

Lyle's "Alpine Meadow"

Dr. Hotchkiss is a graduate of the University of Michigan, baby-boomer, musician, author, and retired dentist. The Changeover is his fourth publication. The Changeover is the fruition of a lifelong professional and personal search for answers to difficult questions, especially how to successfully manage stress, anxiety, fear, and depression. He lives in West Michigan.

www.ingramcontent.com/pod-product-compliance
Lightning Source LLC
Chambersburg PA
CBHW071322140726
47996CB00005B/1769